The Sure Thing

A Pleasure Practice to Revive the Spark

Elana Auerbach

FLOWER *of* LIFE PRESS

"*The Sure Thing* is a sacred reminder that pleasure is not something to earn and shame isn't something to hold us back. Elana's words and practices invite women to soften the old patterns of shame and striving that often keep us from truly feeling at home in our bodies. This book is a reclamation of the feminine, a love letter to every woman who's ready to live fully, freely, and without apology."

—Julie Santiago, founder and CEO of We Are the Women

☆ ☆

"*The Sure Thing* is a wildly entertaining and instructive roadmap to self-discovery, intimacy, and joy. Elana's committed activism, inspired optimism, and practical, down-to-earth advice and exercises made it hard for me to put this book down. For anyone seeking more pleasure in their lives, this book is a sure thing AND a must-read."

—Liz Childs Kelly, award-winning author of *Home to Her: Walking the Transformative Path of the Sacred Feminine*

☆ ☆

"*The Sure Thing* offers a delicious invitation to prioritize pleasure and nourish ourselves through sensual play. Elana has created a deep and whimsical manifesta for radically repatterning our relationships with eros. This book is a blueprint in deepening our sensual and relational capacities."

—Taya Mâ, ritual artist and priestess, co-founder of the Kohenet Hebrew Priestess movement, professor at Starr King School for the Ministry, author

☆ ☆

"*The Sure Thing* isn't just a book—it's an invitation back into your body and your pleasure. Elana has this rare way of making intimacy feel accessible, playful, and deeply sacred all at once. I've read countless books on connection, but this one hit differently—it made me slow down, breathe, and remember that desire isn't something we wait for; it's something we create. If you've ever felt disconnected from your body or your partner, this book will remind you that it doesn't take a miracle to feel alive again—just a little intention and a lot of curiosity."

—Dr. Stacy Friedman, podcast host of Purple Passion Project and clinical sexologist/certified sex coach

"Elana warmly invites you to explore a cornucopia of practices, rituals, exercises, and games that make it easy to go step-by-step from wherever you are now to where you dream of being! She offers a gentle hand to guide you on an empowerment journey, providing a practical guide to erotic self-discovery, sexual fulfillment, and discovering your pleasure potential."

—Sheri Winston, wholistic sexuality teacher, author of *Women's Anatomy of Arousal*, founder of the Intimate Arts Center

☆ ☆

"*The Sure Thing* has more exercises to help people think about, discuss, explore and have sex than I've seen in any other book! I look forward to recommending it to my clients to help them open up more to what it means to explore intimacy with each other."

—Elizabeth Earnshaw, LMFT, author of *I Want This to Work*

☆ ☆

"Instead of sacrificing ourselves and burning our lights out, the practices Elana shares and lives herself give us energy, and remind us that our bodies and hearts are where our power and pleasure lives."

—Christine Arylo, MBA, author of *Overwhelmed and Over It: Embrace Your Power to Stay Centered & Sustained in a Chaotic World*

☆ ☆

"*The Sure Thing* is a brilliant solution to a painful struggle many couples face. After twenty years as a Relationship and Dating Coach, I wholeheartedly believe this book can shift a fizzling sex life into one that not only satisfies, but also supports partners to fall more in love with themselves and each other. I already have couples I'd recommend it to!"

—Shana James, MA, author of *Honest Sex: A Passionate Path to Deepen Connection and Keep Relationships Alive*

☆ ☆

"A must-read for anyone ready to rediscover their spark. I loved the interactive nature of the book; it feels like having a wise, loving friend cheering you on toward more joy and connection. The author's warmth and humor make the topic feel safe, accessible, and empowering. It's more than a book; it's a path to reclaim the embodied pleasure you want. Highly recommended for anyone craving more intimacy and aliveness."

—Laurie Mintz, PhD, psychologist, professor emerita, author of *Becoming Cliterate: Why Orgasm Equality Matters and How to Get It*

The Sure Thing: A Pleasure Practice to Revive the Spark
by Elana Auerbach

Copyright © 2026 Elana Auerbach

All rights reserved.

Without limiting the rights under copyright reserved above, no part of this publication may be reproduced, stored in or introduced into a retrieval system, or transmitted in any form or by any means (electronic, mechanical, photocopying, recording, or otherwise), without the prior written permission of both the copyright owner and the above publisher of this book.

Because of the dynamic nature of the Internet, any web addresses or links contained in this book may have changed since publication and may no longer be valid.

The ideas and suggestions contained within are not intended to diagnose, treat, prevent, or cure any disease or condition and are intended for informational purposes only. Each person's physical, emotional, and spiritual condition is unique. This book is not a substitute for medical or psychological treatment from your own licensed and registered healthcare professional. You should seek professional medical advice before making any health decision.

The views expressed in this work are solely those of the author and do not necessarily reflect the views of the publisher. Neither the author nor the publisher shall be liable or responsible for any damage allegedly arising from the practices in this book. To protect individual privacy, names and identifying information have been changed in stories that include persons other than the author.

Published by Flower of Life Press
www.floweroflifepress.com

Flower of Life Press books may be ordered through booksellers or by contacting:
support@floweroflifepress.com

Cover and Interior illustrations by Gina Sawaya
Cover and Interior design by Jane Scott Ashley

Library of Congress Control Number: Available upon request.

ISBN: 979-8-9987870-7-2

Dedication

To LOVE—that mysterious force that softens my heart, opens my mind, and makes me a better human.

Contents

Note from the Author

The Big Picture—Can a Weekly Pleasure Practice Change the World?

A few months before this book was due for publication, a friend asked if it was part of a bigger vision—some larger project it might belong to. Her question gave me pause. What could it be? I found myself wondering if this book could serve as a bridge to another abiding passion of mine: that of creating a kinder and more just world.

It was twenty-five years ago that I first became acutely aware of the immense social privilege my white skin grants me. The year was 2000, and I was in Baltimore for a weekend workshop called "The Bridge Experience," an experiential deconstruction of race and power led by two Black men. There were chairs set up in rows, like seats on a bus. The facilitators asked us to choose a seat—front, middle, or back, based on our perception of our social privilege. Without much thought, I walked toward the back of the bus. Then I looked around. Most of the other participants seated there were people of color. I realized that my personal history—with its experiences of disempowerment and feelings of inadequacy—maybe wasn't as relevant as I'd thought. My privilege was undeniable. I turned and walked to the second row, figuring the first row belonged to straight white men.

That workshop changed me. I began seeing the world in quite a different way. One particular practice I established from that training was to stop and witness whenever I saw the police engaging with a person of color. I knew that my simple presence could change their behavior.

A couple of years later, at a lecture, I met a Palestinian man who grew up in East Jerusalem. I am Jewish and was raised a fourth-generation Zionist. This was the first time I'd heard a different narrative about the Holy Land. It shook me, and I realized there was more to learn. I joined a Jewish-Palestinian dialogue group and began a lengthy journey of untangling Zionism.

Then in May 2020, George Floyd was brutally murdered by police. This was another rude awakening for me. The racism and white supremacy intrinsic to our society was undeniable. I made a personal commitment to do all I could to end white silence. I figured it made sense to start right where I was, so I began to research the Berkeley Police Department. I learned about Kayla Moore, a transgender Black woman who was killed in her own apartment in 2013. Berkeley police had responded to a crisis call—she had a public record of mental health challenges—and she died with a handful of police on top of her.

How could I have not known about this, having lived in Berkeley since 2006? I was dismayed by my ignorance and realized I needed to educate myself further on these matters. And the more I looked, the more injustice and inequity I saw.

That's when my inner activist came to life in technicolor. I joined Berkeley Copwatch, regularly attended city council meetings, and advocated for tenants' rights, housing justice, and community-centered public safety.

Months after diving full tilt into the world of civic engagement, Bill and I started our weekly Sure Thing practice. The timing could not have been better. Suddenly, I had a practice to fuel me—and my activism—with love. Our Sure Thing became the well I returned to, reminding me that authentic change—the change I longed to see in our world—must be rooted in love.

As man-made atrocities flood our social media feeds and authoritarianism takes root around the world, it's hard not to feel our hearts battered daily by fear, rage, and grief. Meanwhile, in order to actualize the world we dream of, we must be informed, active participants. But how do we tend to ourselves in the process?

In a sense, I believe we've been primed by these times—our hearts are already shattered open. So, what if we consciously fill them with love? Suppose we intentionally cultivate more joy, ecstasy, and pleasure? There is plenty of science to back this up: pleasure actively resources the nervous system, and joy sustains us for the long haul.

How many people practicing a Sure Thing would it take to tip the scales? Could a weekly focus on intimacy and connection prove a genuine antidote to a reactive, polarized, and domination-centered society? Could a regular pleasure practice help create a world based on kindness, collective well-being, and the sanctity of all life? Is there a threshold number of Sure Thing practitioners that would be the tipping point for palpable, positive change in our communities—and our world?

The Sure Thing pleasure practice takes activism to the next level: fill up your bliss bank and then direct the overflow into your relationships, your community, and the planet. To make this easy and fun, at the end of each chapter, you'll find a "Love Ripple," a micro-challenge for you—one small, doable action designed to spread the love from your heart out into the world.

How many love ripples would it take to create a tsunami of love powerful enough to awaken the heart of humanity? One thing I know for sure: We won't know unless we try!

That's why I started the Sure Thing Love Experiment. Curious? Fabulous. Join the growing movement at:

www.surethingexperiment.com

THE SURE THING
GLOBAL
love
experiment

Preface
Let's Get This Party Started!

Dear reader, I offer you a heartfelt welcome to this journey into pleasure and intimacy. For some, this may be your very first foray into the world of intentionally exploring pleasure. Shehechiyanu![1] For others, you may already have a sex life with a lot of pleasure. And still others may be somewhere in between. Wherever you are, welcome!

My hope is that this interactive playbook will make your journey into pleasure as accessible as possible and inspire you to start a weekly practice. Some may wonder: Why bother having a weekly pleasure practice?

I believe we could all use more pleasure in our lives. More connection to our bodies, to ourselves, and to each other. So whether you're single or in a relationship, if you're frustrated with your sex life, want more sensual satisfaction, and have yet to discover a way to reliably get it, a Sure Thing practice is for you.

If you're feeling stressed out, unfulfilled, or numbed out—like you're just going through the motions—and you want a catalyst to reconnect you with that spark of life you know is inside of you, a Sure Thing practice is for you.

And if you already have some sort of regular practice in your life, even better. Whether it's meditation, exercise, yoga, martial arts, hiking, journaling, or therapy, you are someone who already recognizes the benefits of having a regular practice. And I promise that adding a weekly pleasure practice will bring more *vavoom* into your life!

Okay, sure, sounds great. But who has the time or energy for that?

Good question. What I can say is that while this practice will take some time, it will actually add energy to your life. A Sure Thing practice has been one of the greatest gifts I've ever given myself. That's why I wrote this playbook—in short, to share the love.

In a world filled with conflict, polarization, and human suffering, having a practice that creates more connection and pleasure is a worthy endeavor. In the words of Burt Bacharach: "What the world needs now is love, sweet love." And that's what a Sure Thing practice will do. Bring more love into your life, your relationship, and the world.

A Sure Thing practice is a love-replenishing practice. Whether it's self-love or love with a partner, a Sure Thing practice will re-ignite the sizzle that once was or illuminate something you never knew was there. This playbook acts as a cheerleader for you to get to know what it is you really, really want, so that you feel satisfied, turned on, and in unconditional love with *you*.

I invite you to take a moment and consider: When was the last time you delighted in the various ways your body moves? Lingered in the subtle pleasure of breathing in and out? Traced a wave of ecstatic sensation as it moved through your body?

Wherever you are on the spectrum of embodiment—whether you barely notice sensation, or you've been exploring it for decades—this practice will lead to discovery, greater intimacy, and an expansion of your pleasure quotient. The universe of pleasure is infinite. And so are the benefits. Intimacy is medicine for the heart, body, and spirit.

As you may have noticed, I call this a playbook. Because this book is interactive, but it's not a *work*book. By taking on the practices recommended here, you will certainly have more play in your life.

This guide will challenge you, inspire you, and ultimately serve as a companion to a lifetime of reliable sensual and sexual fulfillment. So if you're ready to bring more awareness, orgasm, and sensuosity into your life, read on…

What is an Archetype?

"Archetypes assist us in looking at our lives from a much larger, more mythic perspective than our ordinary ego's day-to-day view of the self. Archetypes rise up from the collective unconscious, making their presence known and felt as spiritual reminders that we are more than we seem in daily life."

—Ariel Spilsbury

Archetypes transcend culture, religion, ethnicity, race, and gender. Archetypes are part of the collective unconscious and are accessible to everyone. I first encountered archetypes in the 13 Moon Mystery School, a yearlong journey into the sacred feminine mysteries. Each month for a year, we immersed ourselves in a specific archetype in an effort to understand that particular frequency and connect with our own unique expression of it.

The Goddess of Love, the Great Mother, and the Muse are the archetypes mentioned in this book. Below is a brief description of each so you may more easily access and connect with these patterns in consciousness. The descriptions below are adapted from *The Alchemy of Ecstasy* by Ariel Spilsbury.

✵ The Goddess of Love: She Who Beautifies with Love

Irresistibly magnetizing, the Goddess of Love beckons you to awaken through the senses. She invites you to feel, then respond and beautify. Her way is presence in the present moment. She inspires passion and offers unconditional love and sensual ecstasy. The Goddess of Love sees the Beloved in every face. She creates a perpetual state of harmony. Invoke the Goddess of Love by asking yourself, "What would love do now?"

⭐ The Great Mother: She Who Nurtures and Sustains

Imagine being embraced by a large, soft, unconditionally loving presence. A soothing and inviting sanctuary where you feel loved and accepted exactly as you are. A space where you feel safe to fully surrender and let go. A place of nourishment, gratitude, and renewal. In the arms of the Great Mother, you feel cared for, nurtured, and midwifed through change and growth. Receptivity and nonjudgment are her way. The Great Mother offers exactly what you need to love yourself just as you are.

⭐ The Muse: She Who Plays, Inspires & Creates

The Muse carries the flame of creativity, that flirtatious essence that ignites and catalyzes your imagination. She appears in dreams, visions, and moments of quiet contemplation and whispers inspiration to the creator within. Her whimsically unpredictable presence can be found in spontaneity, play, wonder, joy, surprise, and humor. The Muse shows us that there is no such thing as an uncreative person. Make a date with the Muse and delight in your ingenuity.

Introduction
100% Responsible

Kvetch or create, you choose.

Hot sex in a monogamous relationship of twenty years? Unheard of, right? I thought so too—until I mustered the courage to invite my spouse to be my Sure Thing partner. We do this practice weekly, and on Saturdays—the Jewish day of Sabbath. That's right. We celebrate what I hold to be the holiest day of the week with a most holy and sacred act.

Let me tell you the story of something that happened not very long ago in this galaxy right here…

I don the long silk robe with pale pink roses. Tied at the waist, the plunging neckline exposes decolletage, a thigh peeks out. Feeling luxuriously sexy, I saunter from our bedroom into the living room where he sits on the couch, laptop on lap, engrossed in his work. I clear my throat, and as he looks up, I twirl, the robe billows out, revealing much more than a thigh. He smiles. I reach out my hand, he takes it, and I lead him into the bedroom.

Our Sure Thing playlist[2] is on. I sway to the music as he wraps an arm around my waist and pulls me close. I smell toothpaste on his breath and, wondering if I can taste it, kiss him with a tickle of tongue. As my body softens and relaxes in his arms, a tingle of turn-on shimmers. My hips move closer to his. We rock together to the rhythm.

"What would make you feel more intimate with me?" I whisper in his ear.
"Having sex with you always makes me feel more intimate," he responds, nibbling on my ear.
"Does connecting sensually, not just having sex, make you feel closer to me?"
"Yeah," he says, with a smile.

We only have a few minutes before his work call. I take off his shirt and invite him to lie back on the bed. Then I straddle his hips. The silk robe is the only thing between us. I rub against him. Then, kiss and caress his face and chest. Our bodies melt; the electric current is palpable. We smile. He gives me one last kiss before getting up to take the call.

Now you may be thinking, "Wait, you didn't have sex. No one had an orgasm. How is that a 'sure thing?'"

A Sure Thing practice is created *by you for you*. That means *you* determine what qualifies as a Sure Thing. Our intention is to deepen in intimacy, connection, and pleasure with each other. So even though it was a quickie, I felt juicier in my body and more connected to him than I did before we started.

Bingo!

⭐ Sure Thing in Brief ⭐

The Sure Thing is intended to be a weekly practice. While every once in a while will still reap results, a regular practice will cultivate a depth of self-awareness so you can experience pleasure whenever you want. Beyond the weekly commitment, it's wide open. The Sure Thing can be done solo, with a partner, with a throuple, or with any number of consenting adults. You can spend all night or just 10 minutes on it. This practice is designed to fulfill *your* specific desires, and it can be performed in a multitude of ways. A Sure Thing can involve orgasm, but it's certainly not required. In fact, the only requirement is to satisfy your appetite for closeness and embodied delight.

To give you a few examples…

When practiced with a partner or multiple partners, a Sure Thing could be mutual masturbation, sex of some kind, erogenous zone massage, a shared sumptuous bath, lying next to each other holding hands and noticing how that feels, or even taking pleasure in a meal together.

When practiced solo, a Sure Thing can be listening to rapturous music, any form of self-pleasure, savoring each bite of a meal, or dancing with yourself. Also, for those practicing a Solo Sure, when I give examples and anecdotes about couples, imagine whoever most turns you on as your partner. It could be the divine, a mythic lover, a rockstar, a current crush, or your inner lover. Haven't met your inner lover yet? Not to worry. You'll meet them as you continue reading this playbook.

The only necessities for a Sure Thing are a clear intention and a regular practice. Within that framework, the possibilities are endless.

⭐ Empowerment Through Pleasure ⭐

A few years ago, on a crisp autumn morning, a friend and I were hiking in the hills of Berkeley when she shared a revelation: "I am 100% responsible for my own pleasure."

I loved it! It gets right to the heart of the matter. There's no one to blame, including myself. If I want to have more pleasure, it's up to me to make that happen. I can treat this responsibility like a chore, but then it'll feel like work. Instead, I treat it like a game. When I take 100% responsibility, all of the cards are in my hand, and I get to choose how to play them. It's up to me to make sure I'm having the pleasure I want.

It's true that some lovers have more skills right from the start. Or know how to listen to your body and give you their full attention. Or naturally kiss the way you want to be kissed. But what I've learned is that if there is chemistry, respect, and kindness, sensual and sexual fulfillment are achievable. When I know that I am 100% responsible for my own pleasure, the game is on. But when I don't, I risk falling into old habits of frustration and resentment. More on that in later chapters.

What would it mean for you to take 100% responsibility for your pleasure?

Take a moment and sit with that question. Notice the thoughts and sensations that arise. Do you feel intimidated, maybe some heaviness? Or curious, fluttery, and excited? Or some combination of these? Or something else entirely? Your body's responses will be a crucial ally on this journey of embodiment.

☆ You're the Boss ☆

And, it's not only about pleasure. You're also responsible for setting appropriate boundaries for yourself. You get to say what's right for you and what's not. To feel into your *no* and your *yes*. No one could ever hope to know you as well as you do. That's true as you read this playbook, as you practice your Sure Thing, and as you live your life. You are the ultimate authority on you. If there's a part of this playbook that you don't agree with or don't like, skip it, forget about it, it's not important. Likewise, when you are being intimate with another person, connect with your clearest knowing. Find what's true and right for you. No means no. Yes means yes, until it no longer feels right… and then a *yes* can become a *no.*

You get to say. It's your body. Your pleasure. Your choice.

And if you're not super clear yet on what you want and don't want, what you like and don't like, there are exercises throughout this playbook to help you discover your desires and what's right for you. Your sense of inner knowing will be honed and toned by the end of our adventure together.

The Sure Thing is one way to take 100% responsibility for your pleasure. This playbook will take you on a journey of self-discovery and assist you in creating a personalized pathway to sexual fulfillment. Guided visualizations and exercises, followed by journal pages to write and/or draw your responses and reflections, are included. If you'd rather record your thoughts elsewhere, I suggest you use only one notebook or journal as your Sure Thing chronicle, so everything is in one place.

My invitation is to let this playbook be a companion and guide to a blossoming love affair with yourself and whoever else is lucky enough to practice a Sure Thing with you.

⭐ Overview of this Playbook ⭐

Our voyage begins with the Sure Thing origin story. Then, we'll explore how rituals and practices enhance our lives and support our aspirations. An examination of our puritanical patriarchal society follows and includes how body, sex, and pleasure shaming are not only baked in, but also weaponized. We will shed those shame shackles and break the spell of this toxic narrative with effective and proven strategies. Hallelujah!

Feeling freer, we'll expand both our definition of orgasm and our ability to be with what some consider taboo. Then, you'll meet your inner pantheon: a fabulously fun way to identify and get to know parts of yourself that may be less familiar to you. This will help you to clarify what it is you truly want. Then we'll go on to explore the Solo Sure—because there's no need to wait for anyone else to begin a Sure Thing practice.

We'll get down to the nitty-gritty of what it takes to maintain a sustainable practice: commitment, effort, and devotion. Followed by a variety of ways to warm up and get your juices flowing, along with some of the infinite possibilities of what a Sure Thing practice could look like. Then, we'll explore resistance and the myriad ways to play with it—choosing wise response over knee-jerk reaction. Finally, we'll bring it all together, so that by the end of this playbook, you'll have a roadmap of your deepest pleasure desires, along with a clear plan for actualizing them.

Now that you know where we're headed, let's get busy with the first interactive exercise.

♡ EXERCISE 1: 100% Responsible ♡

First, read through the entire exercise a few times. Then enact it from memory. Do the best you can to recall the specifics of the exercise, but don't focus on getting it exactly right. Allow yourself to surrender to your own inner knowing and guidance as you explore being 100% responsible.

Start by centering yourself and clearing your heart and head. If you already have a practice to do this, please go ahead. Otherwise, I suggest beginning with a 4-1-5 breath.

1. Take a deep breath in for a count of 4 as you focus on the inhale.
2. Hold the breath for a count of 1.
3. Let the breath out for a count of 5 as you focus on the exhale.
4. Repeat until you feel relatively settled and relaxed.
5. Close your eyes. In your mind's eye, allow yourself to review your life as it currently is. Let your relationships come to mind. Notice how you spend your time. See yourself moving through an ordinary day, and then an ordinary night.
6. Notice if there are thoughts or feelings that arise as you review your life as it currently is.
7. If difficult emotions arise, bring to mind a person or animal you absolutely adore—someone who is effortless for you to love. Imagine them sitting in front of you. Allow the love you feel to become a blanket that envelops you. Continue to wrap yourself in kindness and compassion until you are in a place of accepting exactly how your life is. One of my mentors, Ariel Spilsbury, taught me a surefire way to end suffering is to completely accept what is. When we surrender to life exactly as it is, we can make different choices and take action for change. Simple, but certainly not easy.
8. Once you feel open, receptive, and surrendered, allow the words "I am 100% responsible for my own pleasure" to echo in your mind. Notice the thoughts, feelings, and images that arise as you continue to hear these words. Stay here for as long as you'd like.

On the following journal page, write and/or draw anything you'd like to capture and remember. And if you've made it this far, dear reader, you're already well on your way to taking 100% responsibility for your own pleasure. Bravo!

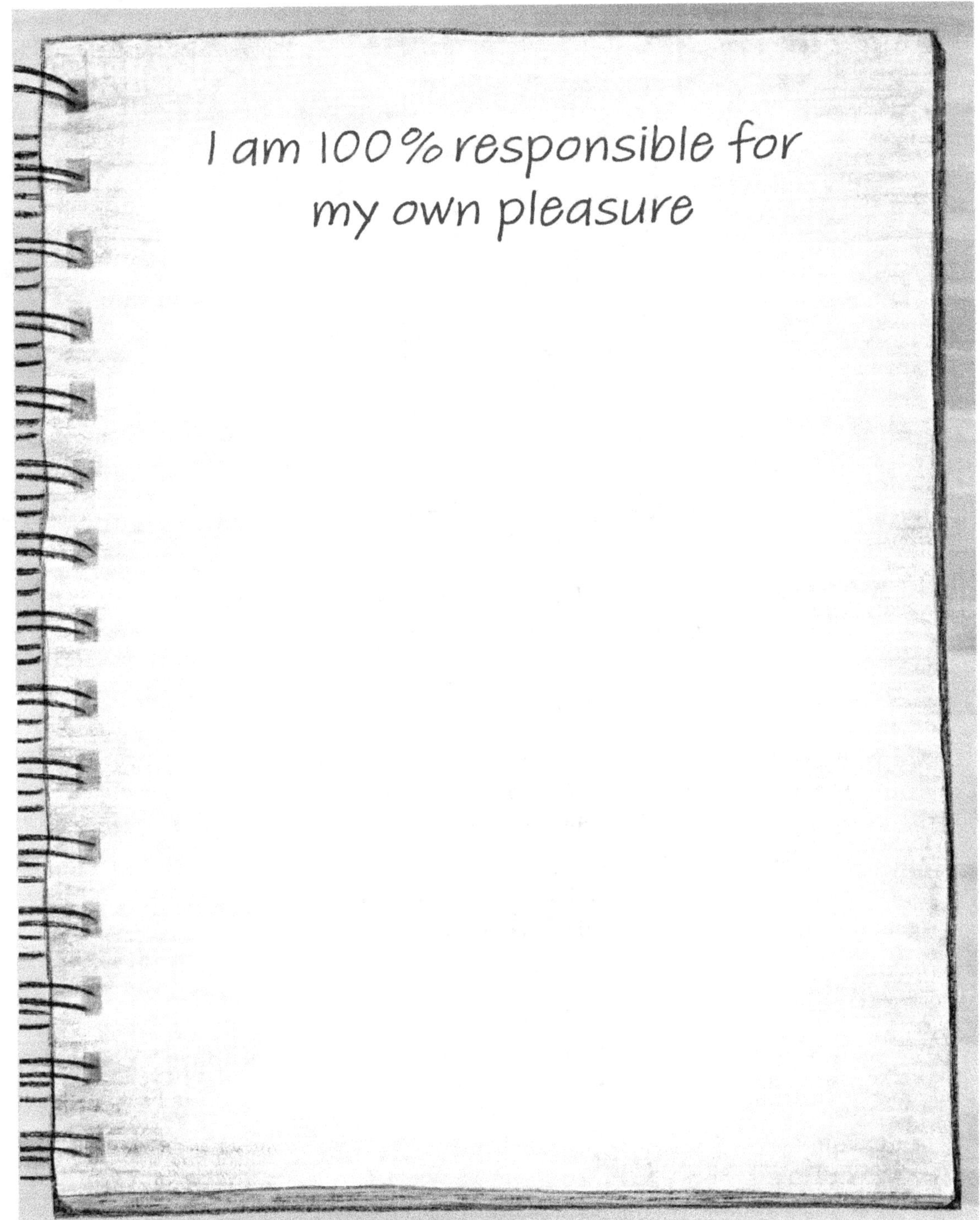
I am 100% responsible for
my own pleasure

Welcome to the Love Ripple!

*"The future belongs to hearts even more than it does to minds.
Love, that is the only thing that can occupy and fill eternity."*
—Victor Hugo

This is the part of each chapter where you get a gentle nudge to be a pleasure activist and bring some good juju into the world. Each love ripple is a mini challenge for you to grow your capacity for intimacy, connection, and pleasure and share it with others. Some love ripples will be easy and others may require you to stretch a bit. As with everything in this playbook, this is an invitation. If what's suggested doesn't feel right for you, change it to something that does.

♥ Challenge

Tell three people in your life something you absolutely love about them. I recommend doing this in person, heart-to-heart, so you can see their response.

♥ Challenge Afterglow

How did they respond? Was it pleasurable for you, anxiety-producing, or somewhere in between? What did you notice about yourself? About the person you appreciated?

No time like the present to begin filling eternity… with love!

Love Ripple Challenge Notes

Chapter 1
The Unfolding of a Love Story

Tending to the heart is like tending a garden—
the more dedicated time and energy invested, the more blossoms.

The idea of a Sure Thing was born in February 2018 during a carpool to a funeral fire ceremony to honor the death of an acquaintance. A woman younger than me had died unexpectedly. She was survived by her spouse and young son. I wasn't close to her, but it felt important to attend her funeral.

Luck would have it—or was it destiny—that a sister priestess[3] who lived nearby was going to the funeral, too. As she drove, I listened to her desire for a consort. She dreamed of engaging in sacred sexuality on Shabbat—the Jewish Sabbath—where we are meant to be in awe and wonder of the Universe. My friend wanted a regular lover to explore with. I learned as a teen that you can earn a mitzvah by making love on Shabbat.[4] What better way to celebrate being alive than by getting it on?

As I listened to her, I felt distinctly turned on. I wanted that, too: reliable, weekly sexy time with my man. That was when it dawned on us: it was a Sure Thing—a Shabbat Unification Ritual!

✩ The Sure Thing ~ An Acronym ✩

The "S" is for Shabbat.

Shabbat is time out of time. Some observant Jews celebrate Shabbat by abstaining from any activity that could be considered work—using electronics, cooking, doing chores, etc. Others study Torah, get together with family and friends, share a meal: the ways to honor Shabbat are as varied as the people who celebrate. Almost 20 years ago, I began a Shabbat practice of not using my laptop on Saturday. Now every Friday evening, I say "Shabbat Shalom" to my laptop for the next 25+ hours. This creates space and distinguishes Shabbat from the other days of the week.

Of course, now I have another Shabbat practice, The Sure Thing, which is an ongoing source of amazement. You don't have to be Jewish or observe any religious or spiritual tradition to have a Sure Thing practice. And, a Sure Thing doesn't have to happen on a Saturday. Just like everything about a Sure Thing, it's designed to suit you: your desires, your schedule, and your appetite.

The "U" is for unification.

You are part of the whole. It's true. Each one of us is an integral and intrinsic part of all that is. Unfortunately, most of the time we're not aware of our interconnectedness. The unification part of this practice refers to that knowing becoming palpable, something you experience in your body, feel in your heart, and know in your bones. You *are* part of the oneness of all that is. When you practice a Sure Thing, you invite an experience of integrating all parts of yourself, merging with a partner, and perhaps even uniting with the divine.

Finally, "R" is for ritual.

A ritual is something done regularly that can transform the ordinary into the sacred. We'll delve into rituals in Chapter 2.

Before we go any further, I want to tell you a story.

Growing up, I was the quintessential good girl doing the bidding of my parents, my teachers, or some other authority figure. Among my "accomplishments" before the age of 25: graduating from UCLA magna cum laude with a double major in math and economics and a Wall Street job in investment banking.

In the mid-1990s, while working in New York City, one of my colleagues set me up on a blind date. The guy seemed like a perfect match, on paper anyway. He was handsome, kind, financially successful, and someone whom my parents would come to adore. That I felt no chemistry with him was irrelevant. After an appropriate courtship, we were on a beach in Florida. He knelt on one knee, pulled out a velvet box with a rock and proposed. I was nodding in response even though a volcano had erupted in the pit of my belly. Something inside was screaming "NO!" I ignored it. I didn't want to hurt him. And, I had yet to experience soul-satisfying sex and true intimacy. So I ignored my body's guidance, tolerated the situation, and continued riding the conveyor belt of life.

A few years later, in my early 30s, I knew I had to get out of the marriage. We had been to every kind of therapy imaginable. I kept trying to find a place in my heart for him. The problem was, he was already in my heart; it was my pussy who couldn't be bothered with this guy.

Along with couples counseling, I'd also started the Hakomi Method, a form of mindfulness-centered somatic psychotherapy. One day, I did a medicine journey with my therapist, and something colossal shifted. I decided I was done playing nice. Done hiding my needs. And my lust. That night, in the den of our quaint San Francisco home, I left my marriage.

A couple of months later, a friend was hosting the Pleasure Course at her bougie apartment in Pacific Heights. What a perfect way to explore my newfound sexual freedom. The workshop was fun. At the end of it, I signed up for the Advanced Pleasure Course a few months later. In the days leading up to it, thoughts like "You've already done this," "What more could there be?" and "You're wasting your time and money" plagued me.

Since I'd already paid the non-refundable fee, I figured I might as well attend. The morning of the course, I arrived early. I walked up a flight of stairs to the second-story apartment in the Inner Sunset neighborhood of San Francisco. The front door opened onto a nice-sized living room with flower bouquets and cushions arranged throughout. Downtempo music played softly. Feeling awkward and wanting something to do, I went to get a cup of tea.

In the small rectangular kitchen, fluorescent lighting glinted off the linoleum floor. A man stood in the middle of the room. As our eyes met, everything melted away and only our locked gaze existed. I felt like I knew him, though we had never met before. The chemistry was undeniable.

When the course leader asked us to find a partner, a zing of heat shot up my spine. I knew exactly who I wanted. Bright blue eyes, shy smile, wild hair—it had to be Bill from the kitchen. Coyly, I looked out of the window, pretending to be fascinated by the tree outside. After a beat, I turned back to see Bill smiling and gesturing me over. We spent the day being led through erotic exercises, culminating in him coming back to my place.

Bill and I officially became research partners—the term used by this hedonistic community of pleasure seekers to avoid relationship or commitment pressure on two people who wanted to explore pleasure together. Sensual and sexual intimacy were explored, but not necessarily an intimacy of the heart. It wasn't about the future. It wasn't about a long-term or committed relationship. Some research partnerships strictly had DO dates (see below) with each other. Others had an arrangement where one person was always the DOer, usually the man if it was a hetero pairing. Still other partnerships explored many ways to evoke sexual pleasure.

Deliberate Orgasm (DO) Date

One person is "at effect" and the other "at cause." The person at effect (let's say, a woman) lies down naked from the waist down. Of course, if you'd prefer to be completely naked, go for it. Another person (let's say, a man) strokes the most sensitive spot on her genitals—her clitoris—with his index finger. By using a combination of strokes, sometimes slower and sometimes faster, he can bring her up and down, helping her to ride what is essentially a roller coaster of sensation. The DOer has his full attention on the sensations in his index finger and allows that to guide him. He may ask questions such as "Would you like firmer

This was radical for me. I'd spent decades accommodating others and dissociating from my desires. My older brother was a needy child, demanding parental attention. I took it upon myself to be the "good girl," never a burden, practically invisible. I always did what was expected of me. In eleventh grade, my father took me out to lunch and, out of nowhere, recommended that I wait to lose my virginity until after high school. Startled into silence, I tried to stuff down the embarrassment with my French onion soup. But the summer after graduation, weirdly compelled by my dad's advice, I was ready to go for it, actual intercourse. My boyfriend was older and more experienced, but he was scared he'd hurt me, and his erection kept wilting. Finally, on a deserted beach in San Clemente, the deed was done. Unfortunately, the waves lapping over my legs was the most gratifying part.

This anti-climactic entrée was followed by plenty of semi-disassociated, mediocre sex through college and into my early thirties. When I met Bill in May 2002, mid-divorce, most everything, including my burgeoning mediation business, took a backseat to my liberated libido. I was discovering what I wanted and how to ask for it. For my 34th birthday, I requested a special celebration where Bill and three others bathed, massaged, and touched me for hours. I was over the moon, able to ask for exactly what I wanted.

pressure? Would you like me to go slower? Do you like this spot better or this spot better?" Simple questions requiring a yes or no answer. The DOee surrenders to the waves of sensation. The DOee may also make requests, such as "Would you slow down your stroke?" or "Would you move to the left a little?" Both people are relaxing, allowing, and noticing. There is no goal to get off in a certain way or even go over the edge, though that could happen. The intention is simply to explore pleasure.

Check out the **Resources** section for more in-depth, step-by-step DO Date instructions.

During this time, Bill and I had an open relationship. We had overt permission to date, make out with, and even have sex with other people. For the first eight months of our relationship, we saw each other only once a week. Bill wanted to take things nice and slow emotionally. This arrangement was challenging for me as I'd been a serial monogamist since I was a teenager. I was used to committing to someone, having them commit to me, and *then* getting to know them. Sounds so backwards when I put it like that.

Even though I felt sexually liberated, I was at my growing edge emotionally. I broke up with Bill just six weeks into our relationship, fearing my needs wouldn't get met. After a session with that same somatic therapist, I recognized I'd been hasty. When I spent time with Bill, I felt met, received, attended to, and adored. As long as I stayed in the present moment and didn't fantasize about what our relationship would become and where things were going, I was good. I tried to emulate the teachings from the book *If the Buddha Dated.*

We were both devoted students of pleasure, with DO dates as our primary exploratory tool. I learned to allow the contractions of going over the edge—often considered climaxing—to be an opening to another level of sensation and orgasmic experience. Going over the edge became a portal into other realms of ecstasy that led to another edge that opened another portal that led to another edge and another portal, and so on. Orgasm became an endless exploration of opening and surrender.

About a year into our romance, we began a daily ritual of Bill stroking my clit. Sometimes I didn't want to, but he insisted, reminding me we had committed to a deliberate orgasm practice. I'd been advised by our pleasure coach to confront any resistance I had to sexual bliss. So I always acquiesced. I lay back with pillows supporting my knees and tried to feel every stroke. Bill was fascinated by the sensations we both felt when he had his index finger on my clitoris. He was a neuroscientist, and now my pussy was his laboratory.

A few months later, Bill made out with a woman who wrote about it in her blog. She described the tingle-inducing scratchiness of his beard as he kissed her back, and although she didn't name him, I knew it was Bill. Many men in our extended social circle were attracted to her. I seethed with rage and anxiety. In a fit of jealousy that lasted about a month, I repeatedly demanded monogamy. Bill finally capitulated. The open door of our relationship slammed shut, but our hot, primal escapades continued, just the two of us.

Then we got married and had a kid. You know the story. There wasn't much opportunity, and there certainly wasn't as much desire, and our cosmic coitus deflated like a spent balloon. Mothering fulfilled me, yet I was still horny at times—I wanted to be ravished and seduced—but Bill just wasn't that interested. He was absorbed in parenting and being our provider. I'd had a brief extramarital affair in my first marriage, and I knew another infidelity wasn't an option. But by the time our son entered kindergarten, my libido had returned full-force, and I needed something. Desperately.

I turned to fantasy and took an etheric beau. One crisp, blue-skied winter afternoon, I went snowshoeing alone and was stirred by the beauty of the bare branches layered with snow. I imagined Pan, the well-hung goat-man, coming to me. I smelled the musk of his skin and felt him devour my neck. Pan turned out to be quite the gifted lover. These fantastical liaisons took place when I was on my own, in the woods. Whenever I wanted him, Pan was there. Surprisingly, I felt physically content after communing with this mythical creature.

But in the end, it wasn't enough. And Bill still wasn't giving me his attention. I became angry, and then resentful. My voice took on a certain tone with him, one that said "you stupid fucking idiot" without actually saying it. One evening while using this tone at our bathroom sink, Bill looked me in the eye and said, "You're being a beeyatch." I was taken aback, then giddy. The spell was broken.

Now that Bill had a way to shatter my bitchiness, he agreed to try something. If one of us was randy, we'd light a candle on the mantle to signal the other to make a move if they felt it too. But the gimmick never worked. When Bill did make advances, I rejected him out of spite for having refused me in the past. He withdrew again. I began overeating. We were stuck in a vicious, not uncommon cycle.

Sexual frustration and dissatisfaction are an epidemic in our society. Studies regularly show that more than 50% of people surveyed are sexually unsatisfied. Even with a multitude of books on the market written by therapists and sexperts, there remains a high level of sexual frustration. Intimacy issues are one of the biggest complaints in long-term relationships. In addition, research shows that most couples consist of one person with high desire/sex drive and one person with low desire/sex drive, which inevitably leads to discontent. This was true for us.

But knowing all of this didn't make it any easier. And even though I loved the idea of the Sure Thing, I was sitting on years of accumulated resentment. It would take many months for me to broach the topic with Bill.

It was December 2020. I was on a hike with Abigail, who told me of the difficulties she was having with her husband. I encouraged Abigail to raise the concerns with her spouse *after* a lovemaking session. Then, it occurred to me, I could do the same with Bill.

For almost two years, I had yearned for a Sure Thing. I needed accountability. I promised Abigail that I'd invite Bill into this practice by the Winter Solstice—the longest night of the year in the Northern Hemisphere that falls around December 21.

As the nights grew longer, I felt a trepidatious excitement. Would he say yes? Of course he would. I didn't really consider any other possibility. If I noticed thoughts like "What if he says no?" bubble up, I would put my attention on what I wanted: more pleasure and intimacy, more orgasm and connection.

The days continued to shorten. My deadline was drawing near. I needed to find a time when we would have privacy. I wanted it to be special *and* I wanted to stay present and in my body when I made the invitation. Would I have the courage to ask him? Could I put aside my anger and blame? I wasn't sure, but I knew I had to try.

It was a Sunday afternoon and our son, now 12 years old, was out of the house for a few hours. This was the moment. I wanted it to be sacred. I needed to ritualize this.

I went to the altar in our bedroom. I said a prayer and I called in courage. I envisioned the fulfillment of my desire. I invoked the archetypal energy of the Goddess of Love. Then, I breathed into my pussy and felt a warm, effervescent energy travel up my body. I lit a candle. The intention to invite Bill to be my Sure Thing partner caressed my lips. Finally, I anointed myself with the luscious scent of rose oil. The ritual was complete.

Bill entered the bedroom. I waved him over to join me at the altar. We stood side by side holding hands. I turned to face him and anointed his heart with the oil.

In the lovemaking afterglow, propped up on an elbow, tummy aflutter, I looked him in the eye. "Hey, babe?"

"Yeah, sugar?"

I'd rehearsed the question several times in my mind already. "Would you join me every Saturday to deepen in pleasure, intimacy, and connection together?"

His face lit up, and he grinned. "I'd love to," he said, and reached between my thighs.

Bill and I have started each day with seated meditation since the beginning of our relationship. I sensed that with a simple structure and both of us being game, change would come. What I hadn't imagined was that the years of amassed gunk between us would dissolve almost immediately. Nor had I imagined that now, in my fifties, a whole new species of seductress would make herself known. Our bedroom became her canvas. My body, her playground. And then she ventured out into the world. Never an athlete, I learned to ski and now train regularly in aikido to satiate her appetite for embodied activity.

It's no longer about the sex. It's no longer even about being in the mood. Instead, I ask myself, "What would make this moment more pleasurable?" Once I have an answer, I might make a request of Bill, turn on a sultry song and let it groove me, or reach for the jar of lube and get myself going. There are no requirements for what physically needs to happen during our Sure Thing, only to relish in our bodies together.

And the Sure Thing has indeed borne out its name. The twelve-year struggle over if and when we're going to have sex is gone, only to be replaced with a sweet anticipation. Every Shabbat, we unearth new sensual terrain. A channel has opened that I hadn't realized existed, and I can only speculate about a line of female ancestors who made love on Shabbat as part of their weekly ritual. As they prepared food on Friday, did they daydream about the sensuous feast they would share with their husbands? Could it be that this practice draws on ancient wisdom, and therein lies its power?

The Sure Thing has been a pathway to genuine self-empowerment for me. May it be that for you, too.

From Cranky to Awed, Just Add Beauty

"Beauty is not in the face; beauty is a light in the heart."
—Kahlil Gibran

Being authentically you is giving yourself permission to experience the full range of emotions. When you feel stuck in a rut of emotional reactivity that you can't seem to shake, use beauty as a tool of transformation.

♥ Challenge

Next time you feel grumpy or irritable, whether it has to do with sexual frustration or not, seek out something beautiful. Find a fragrant flower and inhale; gaze at a piece of art that moves you; go into nature and look at something lovely. Be in the presence of something you find beautiful.

♥ Challenge Afterglow

What effect does beauty have on you? What do you feel in your body? In your mind? In your heart?

Love Ripple Challenge Notes

Chapter 2
Rituals and Practices—Why Bother?

Reality can be shaped with the manifestational tools of intention and attention.

Every morning, as the water heats up, I feel anticipation. I really love my first cup of tea. And honestly, I don't know which I enjoy more, the pleasurable build-up or taking that first sip. Once the leaves are well-steeped, I lift the mug, feeling the weight and warmth in my hands. I touch my lips to the brim and inhale deeply. Nothing quite like the earthy aroma of green tea! When it is cool enough to drink, I take my first sip, my taste buds perking up as the loamy-tasting liquid fills my mouth. When I swallow, a sense of coziness moves down my throat. Still holding the cup, I take a deep breath and observe the effect of the tea on my body and mind.

Prior to picking up the cup, there was me, the cup, the tea—all separate and distinct. Now there is unity. Oneness. Single-pointed focus in the present moment. Everything else falls away, and all I know is the simple, profoundly rich experience of drinking tea.

Sometimes I check my phone while sipping tea. And just like that—I'm no longer present.

What makes the difference? Intention and attention.

✩ Set an Intention, Then Bring Your Attention to It ✩

Setting an intention is giving words to a dream, wish, prayer, or vision. It's like putting a rudder in the river to set the direction you're heading. It's an aim, purpose, goal, or objective. For instance, an intention I've had for many years is good digestive health. To that end, I eat only fruit in the morning and never eat fruit on a full stomach. For my body, this ensures digestive ease.

Once you have a clear intention, bring to it your undivided attention. The mind will wander, of course—that's simply the nature of the human mind—but the more you can return to your intention, the better. Because when intention and attention are combined, our perception of reality can actually shift significantly. These are subtle and potent tools of manifestation.

Perhaps I set an intention before drinking my morning tea to experience each sip with all of my senses. Then, I bring all of my attention to the act of drinking tea. Et voilà! Something as commonplace as taking a sip of tea has been ritualized.

The more I do this, the easier it is to give over completely when I'm drinking tea. Occasionally, I'll find myself consumed by the experience without having set an intention. I think of this as a happy by-product of my ritual. Because the more frequently you bring intention and attention to an action, the more you train your consciousness to spontaneously access a heightened state of awareness.

⭑ What is a Ritual? ⭑

A ritual is one way to animate the ephemeral through consciously connecting the mundane with the sacred. Rituals can be simple and arise unplanned, or they can be ancient and prescribed—or anywhere in between. The two critical aspects are intention and attention.

One example of a ritual is saying a blessing before a meal. Before eating, my intention is to give thanks for the food. It may be as simple as saying "thank you" aloud or to myself. When I'm with others, we might each say one word as we go around the table and co-create a blessing. Or perhaps we hold hands and chant "Yuuuuuuuummmmm." Or we might make something up on the spot. But however we fulfill the intention, our attention is on expressing gratitude for the food we are about to eat.

Many Jewish households have a mezuzah on the upper left doorpost of their front door. A mezuzah is a decorative case containing a parchment with a Hebrew prayer. When I enter and leave my house, I often touch the mezuzah. This ritual reminds me that I'm transitioning between the sanctified space of my home and the outside world. My mezuzah becomes a symbol to bridge the mundane with the sacred, and it rests at a literal threshold.

Anything can be turned into a ritual, even brushing your teeth. An intention could be to release the challenging parts of the day as you clean the plaque from your teeth.

Then, pay attention as you brush. Envision that as the tartar on your teeth dissolves, so do the difficulties from the day. When you're tidying up a room, you might bring the intention of clarifying something that you feel unsure or confused about. As you bring order to your physical surroundings, you simultaneously hold the intention of bringing clarity of mind to an unresolved issue in your life. In this way, literally anything can become a bridge between the prosaic and the mystery.

⭐ Altars Amplify Intentions ⭐

Altars are another way to bring the more-than-ordinary into the day-to-day. Mythologist Caroline Casey's definition of an altar goes something like this: a place where your prayers, wishes, and intentions are symbolized in form. I begin any significant new endeavor with the creation of an altar. This gives me a physical space in which to express my intention to actualize a dream.

An altar can be as simple or as extravagant as you like. The most important part of the altar is that when you look at it, it moves you. You feel inspired. An altar is evocative. Make sure that the altar you create evokes what it is you're going for—beauty, pleasure, turn-on, connection, love, titillation, sensuality, etc. Once you create an altar, it will focalize your intention for as long as you'd like. In other words, you can keep the same altar indefinitely, add to it, and change it as your intention changes. For more on altars and how to create one, check out *Altar Creation* in the *Resources* section.

If you're not feeling inclined to create an altar, try simply lighting a candle and see how that feels.

So, dear reader, we've covered some of the benefits of rituals and how they can aid you in realizing your desires. What about practices?

⭐ Practices Make Anything Possible ⭐

A practice is something done regularly that serves you in some way. Some practices hone and tone your body, others serve to clear your mind and center you, still others connect you with the ineffable and open your heart. There are spiritual practices, such as prayer, meditation, chanting, and visualization. There are physical practices— running, Peloton, pickleball, and swimming, for example. And there are creative practices: writing, painting, dancing, filmmaking, and making music, among others. Then, there are combinations of practices, such as physical and spiritual practices (i.e., yoga and martial arts).

Practices are useful when you want to achieve a goal, get to know yourself better, express yourself more fully, or experience more fulfillment. An altar can aid and enhance a practice. The idea is that when you see the altar, it reminds and hopefully inspires you to engage in that practice.

One of my regular practices is training in Aikido, a Japanese martial art to harmonize energy. With Aikido, there is always at least one place on the body where the two people practicing are touching (i.e., one partner holds the other's wrist or shoulder, one partner holds the other's forearm with two hands). At a recent Aikido seminar, the sensei encouraged us to focus on the physical connection point with our partner. The sensei said that the connection between training partners is always there. Yet when we practice Aikido with our attention and intention on the connection with our partner, that connection is magnified.

A similar phenomenon happens with a fan. Air exists all around you. You know because you're breathing, though you might not otherwise be aware of the air. Imagine unfurling a fan in your hands. Begin to fan yourself with this imaginary fan. All of a sudden, the air is palpable. What was invisible becomes perceptible. Rituals can have the same effect, rendering the impalpable tangible.

⭐ Ritualize a Practice with Intention and Attention ⭐

Remember how a ritual uses intention and attention to connect the everyday with the sacred? You can apply that to your practices, too. A workout can become a way to strengthen your resolve, not just your body—if you set that intention and bring your awareness to it while exercising. A game of pickleball can become an arena for embracing your inner critic, especially when your serve doesn't land where you hoped. Painting or journaling can become a mirror of your unconscious.

I've had a daily Zen sitting meditation practice, called zazen, for over 20 years. Sometimes I ritualize it by lighting a candle and burning incense. The candle illuminates my intention to wake up, and the incense reminds me of all that is unseen. Zazen is a foundational practice for me; it supports me in being open, receptive, and responsive. On the rare morning I don't meditate, I'm often crankier and more reactive that day. Because I know zazen positively affects my state of mind and mental health, most days I get my butt on the cushion as an act of self-love and nurturance.

Let's examine some of the rituals and practices you've already incorporated into your life.

 EXERCISE 2: An Inventory of Rituals and Practices

1. Reflect on the rituals, practices, and routines that you already do (i.e., meditation, walking your dog, making food, working out, therapy, etc.). Jot them down in a list on the following journal page.

2. Now, next to each one, write why you do it—in other words, your intention. For instance, next to "Meditation" on my list, I wrote "grounds me and helps me be less reactive during the day." Next to "Floss Teeth," I wrote "helps prevent gum disease and gum discomfort."

3. Review your list. Place an asterisk (*) on those rituals and practices where your intention is being fulfilled. The ones where you recognize the value of the practice and how it enhances your life.

4. Take notice of the ones that don't have an asterisk. With each of those, ask yourself, "How does this ritual/practice serve me?" Maybe it does. Maybe it doesn't. Be honest with yourself.

5. Is there anything on your list about increasing pleasure? If not, notice whether you have a desire for such a practice.

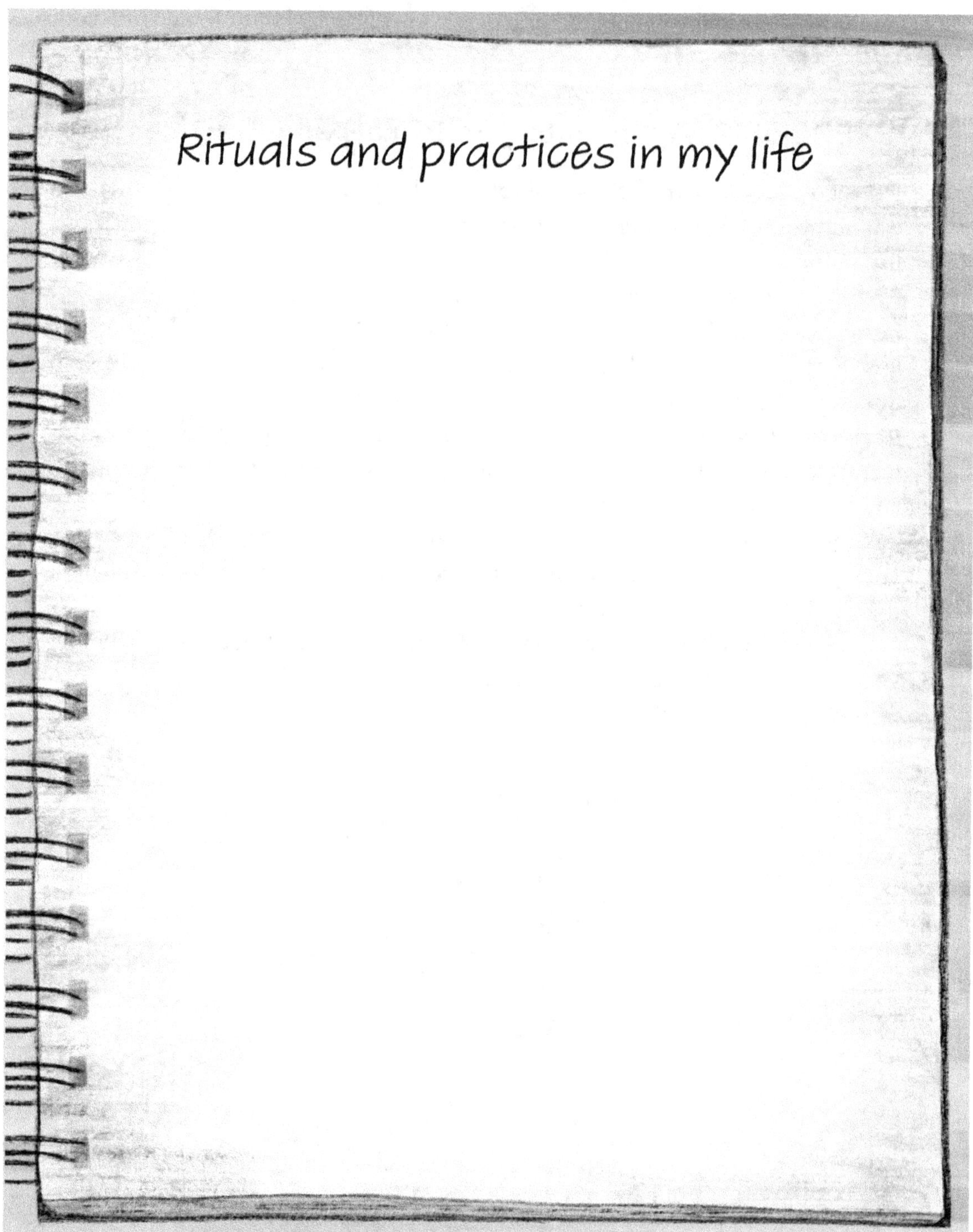
Rituals and practices in my life

⭐ Bridging the Sexual Appetite Divide ⭐

A new practice starts with an inspiration, a new interest, a desire, or sometimes even a crisis. For me, it was a combination of desire and crisis that propelled me to start a Sure Thing. For over a decade, Bill and I were caught in a web of sexual discontent. Until we started our Sure Thing practice, I had no idea how much this dissatisfaction spilled over into other aspects of our marriage.

For years, I used to tease Bill that I'd been duped. For at least the first six months of our relationship, Bill and I saw each other only once a week. That weekly date was usually a sleepover exploring pleasure and orgasm. When we started seeing each other more frequently, we still only made love about once a week. What we would come to discover is that we have different levels of sexual desire.

Research shows that if you are in a long-term relationship, you and your beloved likely experience mismatched sexual appetites. Even though both of you are well within the range of a "normal" sex drive, you and your partner may feel like you are on opposite ends of the spectrum.

You are not alone.

Most couples consist of one person with higher desire/sex drive and one person with lower desire/sex drive.[5] No surprise that these couples are generally not feeling sexually fulfilled. And this often brims over into the rest of their relationship. A vicious and disempowering cycle can develop.

One familiar scenario occurs when the person with higher desire invites sexual intimacy and their partner routinely declines. Over time, feelings of rejection, frustration, and anger can develop in the partner with higher desire. Inevitably, a moment will come when the partner with lower desire feels turned on and makes a move. But past failed attempts at sexual intimacy may lead the partner with higher desire to reject their beloved's advances out of spite.

Another common scenario is that both people just give up and stop trying, which leads to more distance in the relationship, less intimacy, and a consequent nosedive in pleasure. Additionally, there's the possibility of getting one's sexual needs met elsewhere, however briefly, by having a cheat on the side.

Regardless of the details or dynamics in your relationship, if frustration, resentment, and emotional muck are accumulating between you and your partner, you may have unintentionally fallen into an unhappy pattern with no easy way out.

Until now!

 The Sure Thing Pleasure Practice to the Rescue

A simple practice can dramatically alter our lives.

From the first time Bill and I practiced a Sure Thing in December 2020, I felt a shift in me. Over the years that we've had our weekly Sure Thing, I've become closer with myself and with Bill. Our relationship has also become simpler and sweeter, a gift of sensual satisfaction.

I noticed Bill sharing parts of himself he hadn't shared with me before. I was thrilled to be included in his most private thoughts. "What's changed?" I asked him a couple of years ago. "How come after all of the years we've been together, it's only now that you're sharing this kind of stuff with me?"

His response surprised me. "It's because of our Sure Thing," he said. "I feel closer to you than I ever have. There's a depth of emotional intimacy that's grown alongside our sexual intimacy because of our weekly practice. It's opened up new levels of trust for me."

For a moment, I was speechless. I think that may be when it first landed, the subtle power of this practice—of showing up week after week, with intention and attention, in our shared commitment. And a quiet gratitude settled over me.

Priorities

At this point, we've established the potency of rituals and practices. You've identified some that are already enhancing your life. And a Sure Thing practice sounds like something you want. Even so, you may be thinking, "I'm already overwhelmed and over-scheduled. Who has time or energy for this?"

In our troubled world, it's practically impossible to prevent the polarizing energies that pervade our society from seeping into our relationships. If we're not paying attention, the strife of the world—in our communities, our workplaces, our schools, even on the global stage—will find its way into our most important relationships.

It can be difficult to know where to begin when we want to cultivate something different in our personal lives. We have so few examples for how to fall more deeply in love with ourselves and with each other. The Sure Thing pleasure practice is one way to do this, supporting both your relationship with yourself and, over time, the connection with your beloved. If possible, I suggest prioritizing this practice. In my own experience, the rewards begin to show up quite quickly!

⭒ Pleasure Activism[6] ⭒

If you're already an activist, I imagine you're going to love adding a Sure Thing practice to your repertoire. I think of it as a form of activism that animates intimacy and heart opening. As an activist, you see so much that needs to be done to alleviate the suffering in our communities and the world. In order to have the vigor and compassion to serve the needs of others, you must take time to care for your own needs—including the need for connection and physical satisfaction.

Thanks to the joy juju generated from my Sure Thing practice, I am more committed to social justice than ever. I used to waste a lot of time and inner resources on feeling pissed off and sexually dissatisfied. With my weekly Sure Thing, the ever-expanding overflow I feel softens my reactivity and righteousness, inspires new ideas for bringing care and kindness to my community, and nurtures my stamina.

If you've never considered yourself an activist, this is the perfect place to grow your inner activist, given that you'll be taking action to increase pleasure in yourself and your life. As you focus on feeling more good vibes, I guarantee they'll swirl out into the world. Ever been around someone who was so excited about something that it was contagious, and you felt excited yourself? Well, that's how it is with pleasure activism.

But don't take my word for it. Accept the *Love Ripple Challenge* in each chapter of this playbook and taste for yourself what it means to be a pleasure activist.

⭒ Parental Guidance ⭒

And now some extra encouragement for those who are parents with young children.

I get that this may feel like one more thing on an already overfilled plate. I hear you. I really do. *And* I will say that this practice has made me a better parent. I'm able to be more present with my kids. I'm also calmer as the pent-up rage and resentment I used to feel has dissolved.

Of course, there's the question of when. For a while, our son had a drum lesson on Saturdays, so Bill and I took advantage of that hour to have our Sure Thing. If your kid doesn't have a regular time away from you, or you have multiple children, one idea is to enroll a parent friend to start their own Sure Thing practice. Then you can swap childcare duties so you each have your own devoted pleasure time. Or you could just arrange a weekly playdate for your kids.

Another option is to get busy when the kids are asleep, if that works with your schedules and dispositions. Alternatively, you can explain to your kiddo that every week you need privacy to enjoy "adult time" with each other. During those times, your bedroom door will be locked, and you are not to be disturbed unless it's a true emergency. And you can plan a creative project in advance, to keep your child engaged while you and your partner are having a Sure Thing.

Finally, there's always the option of an electronic babysitter! It may be well worth indulging your kids with a little extra screentime so you can have your partner time.

In short: Don't let being a parent stand in the way of you having a Sure Thing. Know that if you want to make this happen, you'll find a solution that suits your circumstances.

And if your daily life begins to feel dull, remember to connect with the extraordinary by creating a ritual. Even the simple intention of taking a deep breath with your full and undivided attention can infuse a moment of wonder into an otherwise hum-drum day.

Now that we've discovered how empowering rituals and practices can be, get ready for an exploration that will take you to your growing edge. Strap in (or on, if that's more your style) and let's dive into the topic of shame.

Sharing a Meal with Intention and Attention

*"Do not be dismayed by the brokenness of the world. All things break.
And all things can be mended. Not with time, as they say, but with intention.
So go. Love intentionally, extravagantly, unconditionally. The broken world
waits in darkness for the light that is you."*

—L.R. Knost

💙 Challenge

While enjoying a meal with others, invite them to join you in an eating experiment. The intention: to savor a bite of food together.

Ask everyone to bring their full attention to this act. To feel the weight of the fork in their hands. Examine the food on the fork. Smell it before placing it gently in their mouths. To allow the flavors to saturate the taste buds. Then chew slowly and swallow consciously. And repeat if desired.

💙 Challenge Afterglow

Did eating in this way enhance the pleasure of the meal? How? Did it cultivate more intimacy?

Love Ripple Challenge Notes

Chapter 3
Shame on Who?

Reserve the phrase "I'm sorry" for when you want to right a wrong. Disrupt the habit of apologizing for simply being. As you catch yourself saying "I'm sorry" when you bump into someone or some other inoffensive act, correct yourself with, "I mean, I'm STARRY." Because you are!

⭐ Body Positivity ⭐

For over a decade, I led a year-long training for the Sanctuary of the 13 Moon Mystery School. Each month, there was a different sacred feminine archetype to connect with and embody. We would focus on one of 13 archetypes (i.e., the Great Mother, the Goddess of Compassion, the Initiator, the Wise Woman, more on archetypes on page xvii) to find our own expression of that energetic pattern. When it was the Primal Goddess month, our outdoor ceremony began around a big fire with drums beating. We invited our wild, innate, instinctual selves to come out and be seen. Some in the group were instantly comfortable with the vibe—their clothes came off as they danced around the fire with abandon. Others had to work their way there.

My attention was particularly caught by two women in the group, Freida and Doreen. Both grew up in the same country in the Middle East. Freida was unabashed in her expression of the Primal Goddess, while Doreen remained clothed, her body language contracted. Doreen couldn't understand how she could have such a different response from Freida, having both grown up in similar environments, including religiously.

How was it that Freida had come to accept her body just as it was while she, Doreen, was awash in shame?

Freida was thin and petite, while Doreen was larger-bodied and buxom. As the layers of shame dissolved throughout that day, Doreen had an "Aha" moment. On top of the sexual repression she'd inherited from her culture of origin, she had internalized Western ideals of beauty. Doreen's focus on what she was *supposed* to look like prevented her from accepting and loving the body that she actually had. By our evening ceremony, Doreen was dancing freely and enjoying her gorgeous body temple.

Body positivity means embracing and celebrating different body shapes and sizes. I see it as the foundation of sex positivity. Sex positivity means treating sex as a normal, healthy part of being human. It means respecting others' sexual preferences and consensual sexual activity. It's about a positive attitude toward sex, rather than sex being a taboo topic or a source of shame.

⭐ Patriarchy, Puritanism, and Pleasure ⭐

Perhaps you're lucky enough to live in a place or community that is sex positive. But even if you live in a sex positive place, you may not be surrounded by people who consider sex something to be honored and celebrated as a natural part of our human expression. You may also have grown up with influences that didn't accept and value diversity in body type. The fact is, negativity around sex, pleasure, and our bodies is baked into the dominant cultural narrative of patriarchy and puritanism.

We're going to delve briefly into this disempowering story in order to see it for what it is—*simply a story*—so we can move past it.

Patriarchy is a paradigm that centers maleness and hierarchy and goes back thousands of years. In ancient Mesopotamia, Hamurabi's Code (c. 1754 BCE) established a social structure where men held authority over women. In ancient Rome (c. 753 BCE–476 CE), the paterfamilias, or eldest male of the family, had absolute authority over all family members, including women and children. In the 16th and 17th centuries, women dubbed witches were burned across Europe and the American colonies. And these are just a few examples.

A primary manifestation of patriarchy is "power over" rather than "power with." When examined, this describes most of the institutions in political and economic life today. Depending on your personal history and ethnic, religious, or cultural background, you may have had different degrees of experience with overt patriarchy. It is very likely that your life—including your sense of self-worth—has been influenced by this pervasive dominant narrative. Take the gender pay gap as an example. In

2024, women in the U.S. earned 81 cents for every dollar earned by men. The Equal Rights Amendment, which guarantees gender equality as a constitutional right, was first introduced in Congress over a hundred years ago. But it has yet to be passed.

In addition to patriarchy, puritanism is another key word here. The Cambridge Dictionary defines it as "the belief that it is important to work hard and control yourself, and that pleasure is wrong or unnecessary." The Puritans were members of an English religious reform movement who migrated to New England in the early 17th century. These folks set the foundation for the religious, intellectual, and social order of the so-called "New World." Aspects of Puritanism still reverberate in American life today. Breastfeeding, for example, was illegal in public until relatively recently. New York was the first state to protect public breastfeeding in 1984, and it took almost 40 years to legalize it in all 50 states. Legislation attempting to dictate what people can and can't do with their own bodies (such as anti-abortion and anti-trans bills) are examples of initiatives rooted in a patriarchal and puritanical worldview.

⭐ Shame is Weaponized ⭐

Along with causing active harm, puritanical patriarchy instills shame and fear in us. Shame is intrinsically repressive, and it's used to try to keep us silent, obedient, and confined. It's similar to the age-old patriarchal strategy of divide and conquer, which is sown in fear. This strategy manipulates people to ensure they're in continuous conflict with one another, rather than turning their attention and collective power against the ruling elites to create a truly just society. We see this when the powers-that-be instigate tensions between working-class whites and people of color, as well as in anti-immigrant narratives.

Shame is exploited in a similar way to fear. The difference is that instead of turning on the "other," we turn on ourselves.

Much of this comes through the media. We are bombarded with expectations of what is considered attractive. Everywhere you look—social media, fashion magazines, billboards, advertisements—beauty is portrayed in a specific way, with an extremely limited lens. Advertisers prey on our fears that we aren't enough—we're too fat, too old, too unattractive, too whatever it is that will make us believe we're not good enough exactly as we are. In this way, we're manipulated to believe we're in need of whatever is being peddled—fad diets, trendy workouts, Botox, blonder hair, anti-wrinkle and cellulite products, cosmetic surgery… the list goes on and on.

This conditioning is used to bamboozle us into spending our attention, energy, and resources on attaining some superficial ideal. And by "us" I especially mean women. We judge ourselves against an impossible standard of beauty—one that is often airbrushed, ironically. We spend countless hours and dollars chasing an elusive dream of perfection.

The sad fact is, shame sells. Collectively, we spend billions of dollars to try to reach some unattainable ideal of beauty. In 2024, in the U.S. alone, $90 billion was spent on weight loss and dieting; over $19 billion was spent on plastic surgery; and $119 billion was spent on beauty products. Capitalizing on our shame for failing to meet such ideals reaps tremendous profit.

Instead, we could be using that time, money, and energy to hone our unique genius, discover our passions, and find genuine fulfillment in our lives.

So why do we fall for it?

⭒ Body, Sex, & Pleasure Shaming: A Brief History of Repression ⭒

In short, these concepts have deep roots. Body, sex, and pleasure shaming have been used by the puritanical patriarchy to suppress us for quite a while. In *Fat Shame: Stigma and the Fat Body in American Culture,* Amy Farrell traces the societal denigration of fatness to the mid-19th century, long before there were any health concerns about a large body size, and well before the diet industry emerged in the 1920s. Farrell claims that fat stigma was related not only to cultural anxieties that emerged during the modern period related to consumer excess, but also to prevailing ideas about race, civilization, and evolution.[7]

For 19th and early 20th-century thinkers, fatness was a key marker of inferiority, of an uncivilized, barbaric, and "primitive" body. This idea that fatness is a sign of a "primitive" person endures today, fueling our $80 billion "war on fat." Anti-fatness stems from the same limited and prejudiced mindset as race science theory and eugenics.[8] In other words, fat shaming is directly related to the slavery-justifying viewpoint that darker-skinned people are inferior to lighter-skinned people.

The first step in emancipating ourselves from these imprisoning perspectives is simply to recognize what is going on. We have to be able to see the prison bars before we can unlock the gate and let ourselves out. Accepting larger-sized bodies, whether our own or others', as just as valuable, worthy, and healthy as smaller-sized bodies is actually a profound act of liberation. Because as we affirm larger bodies, we dismantle racist conditioning and free our minds!

Unfortunately, the story doesn't end there.

Along with being shamed for how we look, women and girls are generally taught to be ashamed of our sexuality. First, there's the double standard imposed on women. A woman who explores sex beyond the usual confines of a monogamous relationship or marriage is often called a slut, her behavior considered socially unacceptable. In contrast, men are often cheered for their sexual adventures. In Emily Nagoski's seminal book *Come as You Are,* along with this double standard, she identifies three core cultural messages about female sexuality.[9]

The Moral Message: This can come in different forms, all stemming from a very old paradigm: You are evil if you want or like sex. Moreover, your virginity is your most valuable asset. Nagoski references James Fordyce's 1766 *Sermons to Young Women:* "Women are appealing when they're meek and ignorant and pure." Clearly, Fordyce and his ilk were at the top of the puritanical patriarchal heap and perpetuating this worldview to maintain their power.

The Medical Message: You are diseased. Nagoski condenses this message as: "Sex causes disease and pregnancy, which makes it dangerous." Nagoski continues: Of course, if you're ready to take that risk, "Sexual functioning should happen in a particular way—desire, then arousal, then orgasm, preferably during intercourse, simultaneously with your partner." When things don't progress in the bedroom in this prescribed way, the message becomes, "There is a medical issue that you must address. With medication. Or possibly surgery."[10]

The Media Message: You are inadequate. In Nagoski's summation: "You're too fat and too thin; your breasts are too big *and* too small. Your body is wrong. If you're not trying to change it, you're lazy. If you're satisfied with yourself as you are, you're settling. And if you dare to actively *like* yourself, you're a conceited bitch."[11]

Taken altogether, it's only logical that this messaging leads to the notion that we should also be ashamed of feeling pleasure. If the female body is intrinsically wrong, and so is female desire, then of course, female pleasure must also be wrong.

⭐ Shame vs. Guilt ⭐

Shame is different from guilt. Guilt (or regret) arises when we've deviated from our internal sense of morality. For instance, losing your temper and saying something awful to a loved one in the heat of the moment. We've all done it. We may regret what we said or even feel guilty for saying it. This experience gives us the opportunity to reflect, make amends, and try to do better next time. Feeling regret or guilt brings the opportunity for growth.

In contrast, when we feel shame, we experience guilt or regret but then add another (imagined) person's judgment onto our actions. Shame is something from the outside that gets put on us.

The judgments that give rise to shame might come from an individual. For example, if you were caught pleasuring yourself as a child by someone who was sexually closed and then they shamed you for it. You may have thought you were "bad." When we experience shame as an adult, it's typically because we have internalized these judgments.

The judgments that give rise to shame, though, can also be cultural, such as buying into a toxic cultural narrative or the patriarchal puritanism described previously.

⭐ Shame Shuts Us Down ⭐

On the level of the nervous system, shame works to shut us down, so we can't see any options. Dr. Stephen Porges' polyvagal theory suggests that the involuntary nervous system's response to shame is not limited to fight-or-flight but also includes a social engagement system and a shutdown response. Shame often results in social disconnection and self-isolation, which in turn activates the body's shutdown response. Thus, shame becomes a self-fulfilling loop of disassociation, where a quick-fix, surface-level solution is sought to assuage the loneliness and unease. Getting the latest glossy product may make you feel better temporarily, but it won't free you from the shackles of shame.

⭐ Pleasure Liberates! ⭐

There's good news. Recognizing how we've been manipulated by the false narrative of the puritanical patriarchy disrupts the disempowering cycle of shame. That's when genuine autonomy and self-empowerment can emerge. We can liberate ourselves from the shame we carry around our bodies and around sex itself, using pleasure as our lodestar.

Imagine a childhood where you were encouraged to revel in the wonders and pleasures of your body, in an age-appropriate and sex-positive way. Imagine an adolescence where you were taught to love and befriend your genitals. To discover what felt good to you, how you liked to be touched, and how to communicate that to another person. Where you were taught how to understand your own body's signals and inner guidance so you could set healthy boundaries. An adolescence where you learned that everyone's genitals were unique and perfect, just as they are.

Now, dear reader, I ask you to go a step further and envision an entire culture where we recognize that our bodies are innately sensual, and that sexuality is a glorious expression of our humanity and our interconnectedness.

Isn't it beautiful? And liberating?

Another world is indeed possible!

All that said, let me remind you, as you make your way through this playbook, you are your own best authority. You are sovereign. You set the pace, and you say what's right for you. I may give a little nudge here and there, but you're the one at the helm.

Join me in an exercise?

♥ EXERCISE 3: Shedding Shame Shackles ♥

First, read through the entire exercise a few times. Then enact it from memory. Do the best you can to recall the specifics of the exercise, but don't focus on getting it exactly right. Allow yourself to surrender to your own inner knowing and guidance as you shed the shackles of shame.

1. Center yourself with the 4-1-5 breath (This is explained in more detail in Exercise #1 on page 6. In brief: Breathe in for a count of 4, hold the breath for a count of 1, breathe out for a count of 5) or any other way you'd like to center yourself.
2. Bring to mind a situation where you were being shamed. Whether you were a child, a teen, or an adult, allow yourself to really remember this experience.
3. Close your eyes and take yourself back to that scene. Allow yourself to recall as many details as possible. Where were you? Who was there? What was happening before the incident? How did you feel? What provoked the shame?
4. Immerse yourself in the shame as much as feels wise. In response to feeling ashamed, how did you react? What did your body do? What did you think? How did you feel?
5. Now, recall that shame is used to make us feel inadequate, inferior, and alone. Let the adult, resourced part of you—I like to call this part the Great Mother—bring that understanding and awareness into your experience of feeling shame. What happens? Notice any new thoughts, feelings, and responses. Perhaps, in your mind's eye, the memory changes. Perhaps you even see yourself acting differently. Let yourself steep in this "new memory."
6. Before opening your eyes, envision yourself underneath a waterfall of light. See, sense, and feel this waterfall seep into every part of your mind, heart, and body. Saturate yourself in this cascading energy of light, allowing yourself to feel revitalized and whole just as you are.
7. Feel the Great Mother embracing you in Her unconditional love. Wrap your arms around yourself so that you viscerally feel hugged. Remember you are loved just as you are.

Whatever feels important to capture and remember from this exercise, draw or write it in the following journal page.

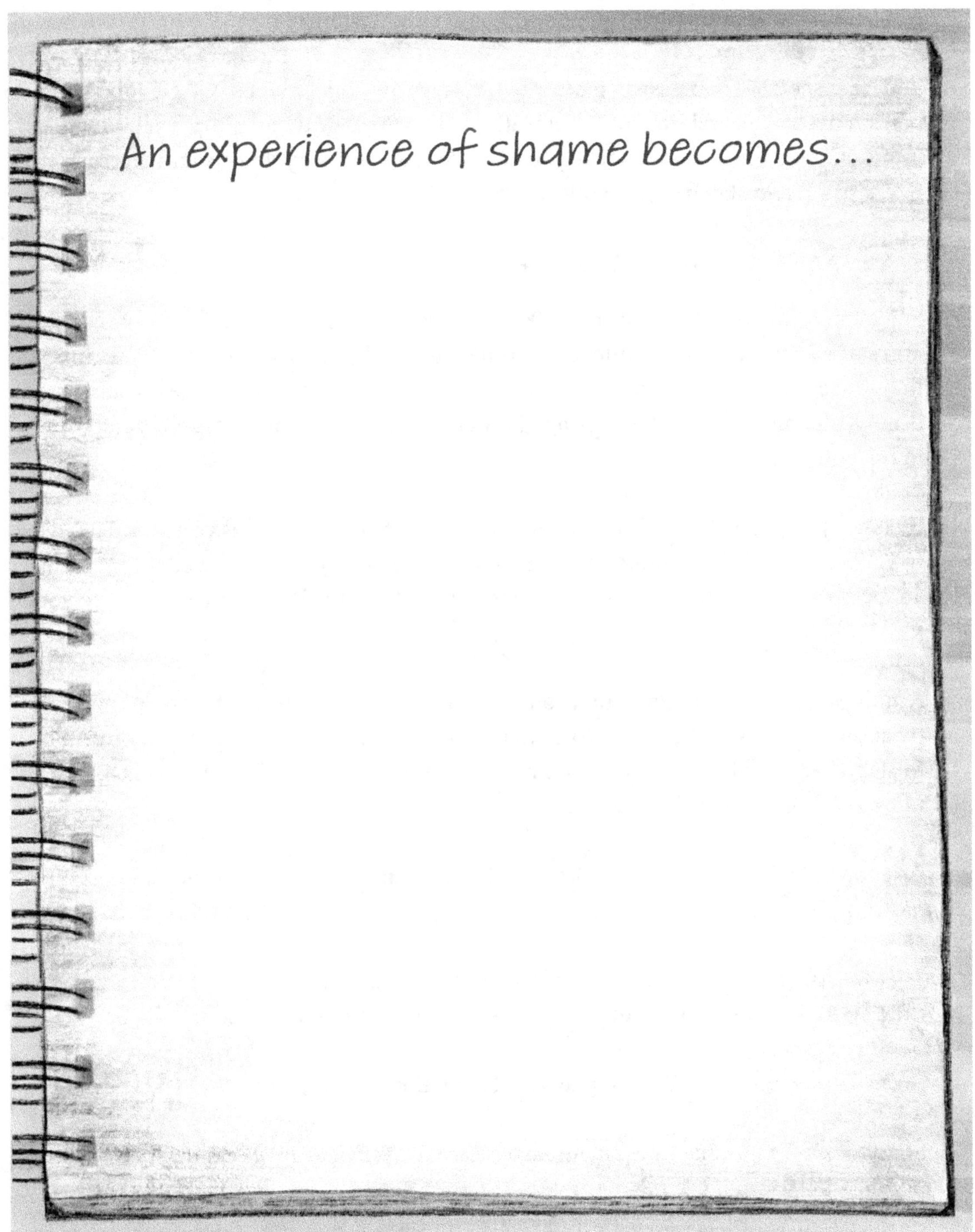
An experience of shame becomes...

Now, if someone attempts to shame you, you have options.

You can see the oppressive pattern more clearly and choose not to follow the patriarchy down a rabbit hole of negative self-worth. You can simply reply with a pithy, "Shame on who?" And, if you do get caught in a cycle of shame, return to Exercise #3, and shed those shame shackles.

⭐ Name the Shame: A Game ⭐

Since I met my inner activist in 2020, I've been organizing with many people on an array of issues from actual affordable housing for all, to shrinking the footprint of the police, to a free Palestine. When the idea of the Sure Thing Love Experiment occurred to me, a flash of telling one of my activist friends about it caused a clutching in my gut.

I felt her judgment. Then, I imagined her saying with a tone of dismissal and an eye roll, "Pleasure? How frivolous at a time like this. There's work to do. People are being abducted, starved, killed. How can you think of pleasure? What a privileged life you lead."

Amidst a barrage of judgmental thoughts, I realized those thoughts weren't coming from someone else. That was a voice in my head. Shame was trying to get a foothold to stop the flow of creativity. To get me to drop this project. To keep me "safe" and not risk being criticized or demeaned.

As soon as I named it, I saw it for what it was—an attempt to smother and repress passion.

That was the first time I played the "Name the Shame" game. A week later, I was on the phone with my mother-in-love, and she said, "I'm embarrassed to tell you."

"Wait," I interrupted. "Want to play the 'Name the Shame' game?"

She chuckled, then shared what embarrassed her. With a little playfulness, the shame became intimacy.

Whenever I sense humiliation, I now have a way to play with it. And is it ever freeing to say, "I feel embarrassed by what I did." Or "I'm ashamed of what I said." Or "I'm afraid you're going to judge me, but I'm going to tell you anyway."

⭐ The Rules ⭐

1. When you sense shame, in yourself or someone else, take a deep breath and greet it. "Hello, Shame. It's been a minute."
2. Then, discern whose voice it is. A parent, an authority figure, the puritanical patriarchy, a voice inside of you?
3. Who are you afraid will judge you? Are you judging yourself?
4. Name the shame!
5. Notice how you feel.

Finally, let's not get caught up in the shame fest that political, activist, and other spaces can devolve into. Yelling "Shame!" at someone isn't helpful. It won't change their behavior, and it could have them dig in their heels. Regardless, when we go there, we become part of the toxic narrative we're trying to ditch. Instead, demand what you want (i.e., Justice! Transparency! End All War!) and live the new story we're co-creating.

Now that the proverbial elephant in the bedroom, shame, has been outed, let's dive into orgasm.

Into the Daylight with You

"Shame hates it when we reach out and tell our story. It hates having words wrapped around it—it can't survive being shared. Shame loves secrecy."
—Brené Brown

Ever notice how most people are wearing the same style of clothing in similar colors? There's an unspoken dress code to blend in and not draw attention to yourself. Maybe a remnant of the puritanical patriarchy?

♥ Challenge

Find an item of clothing that you feel a bit uncomfortable wearing in public. Perhaps it was an impulse buy, or a friend convinced you that bright color was fabulous on you. Regardless, what is clear is that you'll be receiving attention when you wear it.

Don the garment and go out on an errand or summon the nerve to wear it all day.

For extra self-love credit, play a round of the "Name the Shame" game with someone you encounter. Share the discomfort you felt/feel about what you're wearing.

♥ Challenge Afterglow

Was it easier or more difficult than you thought it would be? Would you wear that item of clothing again?

Love Ripple Challenge Notes

Chapter 4
Redefining Orgasm

Orgasm is one of the most potent energies on earth.

Many define orgasm as the moment when the genitals rapidly contract with a sudden release of tension and, depending on your anatomy, ejaculation can occur. While this definition is accurate from a purely physiological perspective, it's exceedingly limited. And, it involves mere seconds of sensation.

Orgasm can be defined as not only including the genitals, but also the entire body. When I take a bite of something delicious and pause—to allow my taste buds to erupt with flavor, to follow that sensation as it moves down my throat, into my chest, and ripples through my body—I consider myself in orgasm. When I listen to the sound of a flute and my cervix contracts and euphoric energy fills me, I consider myself in orgasm. When my beloved kisses my back and tingles of delight undulate through me, I consider myself in orgasm.

In every moment, I have the choice to enter into pleasure, depending upon where I put my attention. Will I focus on the disturbing thought in my head or focus on a deep belly breath? As my heart shatters at the sight of human suffering, can I include the scent of a rose? When awash in grief and loss, can I feel gratitude for the solidity of the earth beneath me?

To me, the distinction between an orgasmic state and everything else lies in my willingness to fully surrender to physical pleasure. And to allow it to expand. It could be for a few seconds; it could go on and on. I never know. Because there are no limits when it comes to orgasm. Orgasm is one heightened example of pleasure, and pleasure is a vast spectrum of possibilities.

orgasm

According to Ian Kerner in *She Comes First,* studies show that the majority of men—approximately 75%—are finished with sex within a few minutes of starting.[12] On the other hand, up to 15% of women claim they've never even had an orgasm. Many of us have been uninformed or misled about sex, pleasure, and the actual capacities of our own bodies. Whether you're someone who has never experienced an orgasm, orgasms in a matter of minutes, or is multi-orgasmic, redefining orgasm will expand your capacity for pleasure.

In Chapter 2, we examined how bringing intention and attention can transform the everyday into the sacred, the mundane into the magical. This exercise draws on that concept and will help you identify the thoughts, feelings, and beliefs you associate with pleasure and sexual awareness.

 EXERCISE 4: Touching with Intention and Attention ♥

First, read through the entire exercise a few times. Then enact it from memory. Do the best you can to recall the specifics of the exercise, but don't focus on getting it exactly right. Allow yourself to surrender to your own inner knowing and guidance. The intention of this exercise is to pay attention as you touch your body, to notice how it feels, as well as any thoughts that arise.

1. Bring your awareness to your hands as you hold them out in front of you, palms up to the sky.

2. Then, rub your hands together quickly to a slow count of at least 13. Then stop rubbing and slowly move your palms apart. Notice what you sense.

3. Breathe slowly.

4. Gently caress your left hand and arm with your right hand. Use light, tickle-type strokes. Move slowly. Notice what happens.

5. Follow the sensation from the fingers on your right hand, to your left hand, to your left forearm, to your left elbow, and beyond. You may continue to lightly stroke your hand and arm, or perhaps you wish to change the pressure—as you like.

6. As you continue touching, open your awareness to your entire body. Take a deep breath into your chest. Notice how your chest feels as you stroke your arm. Now notice how your belly feels.

7. Do you notice sensation in other parts of your body? Try different kinds of strokes and pressure.

8. Now, focus on your genitals as you continue to stroke your hand or arm. You may observe tingles, energy moving, another sensation, or nothing at all.

9. Finally, notice if any thoughts or beliefs arise.

10. Continue for as long as it is enjoyable, and when you feel complete, write or draw what you observed in the following journal page.

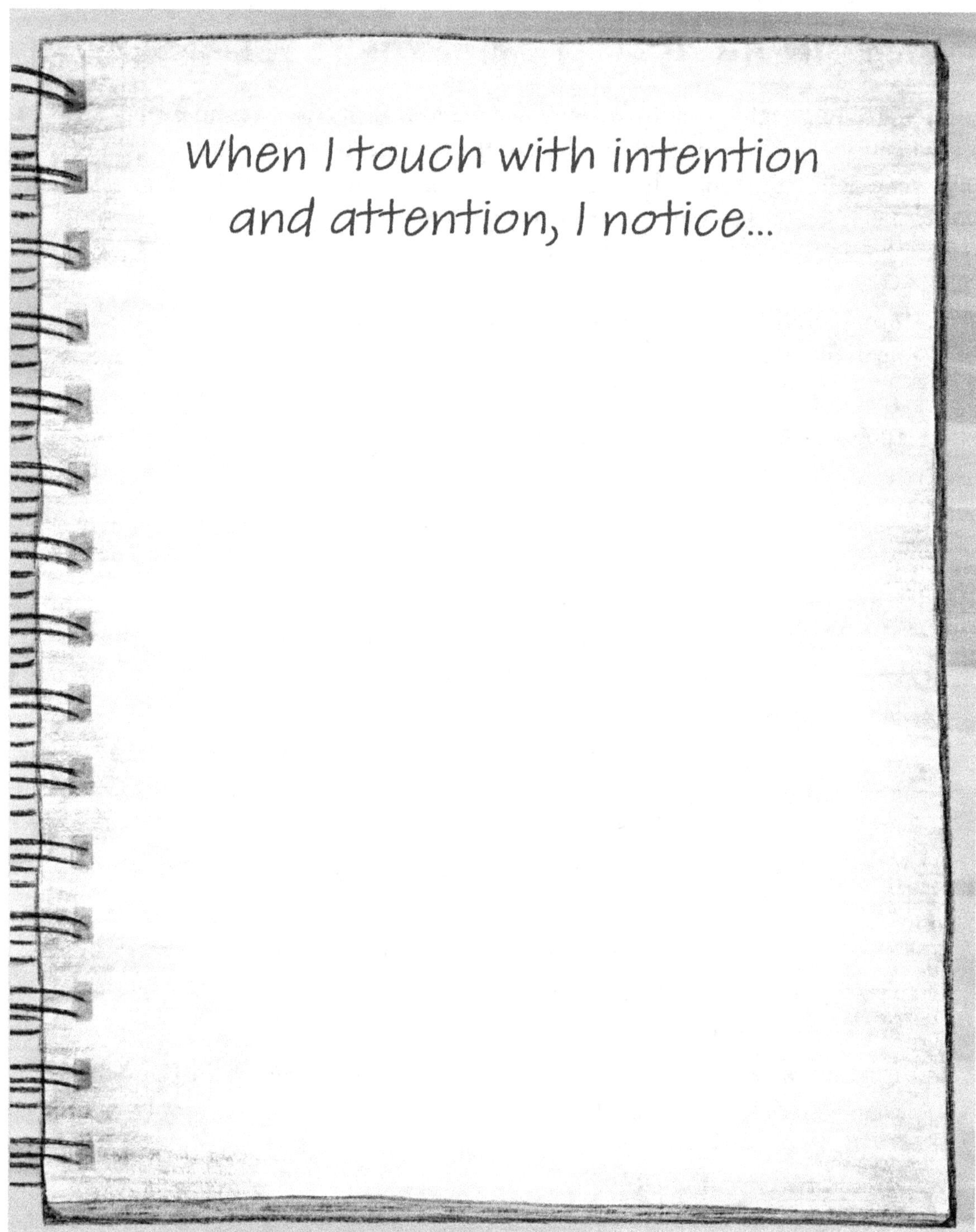
When I touch with intention
and attention, I notice...

As soon as I bring my attention to my genitals, I feel warmth rising up from the base of my spine, and sometimes even a subtle contraction in my vulva. I have entered into an orgasmic state. I'm gently stroking my hand and creating an orgasm in my body!

I encourage you to investigate pleasure in the simplest of ways, and to define for yourself what you consider to be an orgasmic state. It's a fun game to play to see how much pleasure you can have without even touching your genitals.

Which brings us to the subject of genitals. The inner sanctum of pleasure.

⭐ Where? Down There ⭐

Whether you grew up in a sex-positive environment or first encountered the concept of sex positivity in this playbook, we all have names we use to refer to our genitals. The language around sex and genitals can be rife with *do's* and *don'ts*, and often elicits an involuntary reaction in us. Perhaps you use the term that the adults around you used when you were growing up. Or maybe you avoid using any term at all and just say "down there." Whatever the case, we are about to confront, in the most intentional and loving way, what is often portrayed as taboo.

Together, we are going to liberate the language of our genitalia. And we're going to step through this gateway consciously. So whether you feel titillation, dread, excitement, curiosity, boredom, or anxiety… it's all good. The key thing is to notice the thoughts and sensations that arise.

If you have a practice to bring yourself into the present moment, please practice it now. If you don't have such a practice, please do Exercise #5.

💜 EXERCISE 5: Entering This Moment 💜

First, read through the entire exercise a few times. Then enact it from memory. Do the best you can to recall the specifics of the exercise, but don't focus on getting it exactly right. Allow yourself to surrender to your own inner knowing and guidance as you explore entering this moment.

1. Find a comfortable seated position, either in a chair or on the floor.

2. Practice the 4-1-5 breath at least three times. (Refer to page 6 for instructions.)

3. Connect with whatever part of your body is touching the ground. Feel the stability of being supported.

4. Envision the gravitational force of the earth as a magnet, drawing all thoughts, plans, concerns, and feelings from your heart, mind, and body into the center of the earth.

5. On the exhale, think/feel/say the word "Empty." On the inhale, think/feel/say the word "Open."

6. Continue for as long as needed until you feel relatively calm and clear.

7. As you notice thoughts or feelings arise, return to the breath: "Empty" on the exhale, "Open" on the inhale.

Now, take a deep breath. As deep as you can. Breathe in through your nose and notice your belly, ribs, and chest expand on the inhale. When you breathe out, notice your chest, ribs, and belly deflate on the exhale. Take at least two more breaths like that. Notice how your body feels. Pay attention to any thoughts or sensations that arise as you read…

Pussy. Cunt. Labia. Vagina. Yoni.

If you dare, say these words aloud. Notice how your body responds. What thoughts do you notice? What sensations? Do you feel tightness and constriction? Or is there openness and receptivity? Do you feel naughty or embarrassed? Do you feel turned on?

However your mind and body respond, allow it. Use this as an opportunity to learn something about yourself. If you feel all warm and tingly in the genital area, breathe into that sensation and see what happens. If you feel constricted, ashamed, or uncomfortable, breathe into it and see what happens. There are no wrong experiences. We are simply noticing how we involuntarily respond to various words for female genitalia.

Then take some time to draw or write your thoughts, reactions, and feelings in the following journal page.

When I read the words
pussy, cunt, vagina, I feel...

Is there a word for the female genitals that you're more comfortable with? If you're game, I suggest you focus on the word that you're most *uncomfortable* with and replace whatever word I use with that word. For instance, if "cunt" is the term that is most confronting for you, when I use a different term for female genitalia, change it to "cunt." I predict that will provide the most interesting exploration of your growing edge. But as always, dear reader… you do you.

Now let's return to presence. Again, use any practice that brings you into the present moment. Please take another conscious inhale and exhale. Notice how your body feels. If you're riled up in any way, wait until your nervous system settles. Then, return to the practice in Exercise #5, or try this one below.

💙 EXERCISE 6: Breath as a Presencing Tool 💙

First, read through the entire exercise a few times. Then enact it from memory. Do the best you can to recall the specifics of the exercise, but don't focus on getting it exactly right. Allow yourself to surrender to your own inner knowing and guidance as you explore the breath as a tool to bring you into the present moment.

1. Get into a comfortable seated position. Breathe normally.

2. As you inhale, say or think, "I am inhaling." As you exhale, say or think, "I am exhaling."

3. Continue this way of breathing until you feel relatively grounded and present.

Now that you feel centered, pay attention to how your mind and body respond as you turn the page and read…

Cock. Dick. Penis. Lingam.

Say them aloud. What do you notice? Do you have the same response as you did to the words for female genitalia, or is it different?

Again, however your mind and body respond, allow it. Use this as an opportunity to learn something about yourself. If you feel all warm and tingly in the genital area, breathe into that sensation and see what happens. If you feel constricted, ashamed, or uncomfortable, breathe into it and see what happens. There are no wrong experiences. We are simply noticing how we involuntarily respond to various words for male genitalia.

Take some time to write or draw any thoughts, reactions, or feelings in the following journal page.

when I read the words
cock, dick, penis, I feel...

Is there a word for male genitals that you're more comfortable with? Again, if you're game, I suggest you focus on the word that you're most *uncomfortable* with and replace whichever word I use for male genitalia with the one that is most edgy for you.

⭐ Pussy & Cock, Sensual vs. Sexual ⭐

In this playbook, I will most often use the terms pussy and cock to refer to the female and male genitalia. Those are the terms that bring me the most pleasure. They produce a little zing in my body when I use them. If these words make you uncomfortable, you may wish to unpack your associations with them. In the meantime, please feel free to swap in whichever terms you prefer. Also, please know that when I use male or female to describe a sensual or sexual act, gender is used as a placeholder; any gender can be used for these exercises.

When we enter the domain of pleasure, energies arise that turn us on and make us feel good in our bodies. These energies could be described as either sensual or sexual or both. Here's the distinction: what I refer to as sensual is the experience of pleasure anywhere in the body. However, when I refer to something as sexual, the genitals take center stage. That is, even if the entire body is engulfed in sensation, pleasure pulsates and expands from the genitals. For example, as I fantasize about my current crush and run my tongue gently over my top lip, that feels sensual. Then, when I bring my awareness to my pussy and continue to lick my lip, I feel subtle contractions in my vulva, and now I'm entering the realm of what I consider sexual.

Finally, I know there are some humans with a combination of male and female genitalia, usually called hermaphrodites or intersex. For you who are blessed with this magnificent biology, my apologies for not having more inclusive language to use. Your emergence is an important part of our evolution as a species. You are intrinsic to our understanding and experience of what wholeness actually means. It is my hope that you know the invaluable gift you offer to the consciousness of humankind.

Ready for more pleasure?

I hope so. Because here comes one of my favorite pleasure exercises!

♥ EXERCISE 7: P-Pump ♥

~a quick and easy way to get some juicy energy flowing~

First, read through the entire exercise a few times. Then enact it from memory. Do the best you can to recall the specifics of the exercise, but don't focus on getting it exactly right. Allow yourself to surrender to your own inner knowing and guidance as you explore the P-Pump.

1. The pelvic floor is a mass of muscle located between the base of the spine and the pelvis. Locate this muscle group by squeezing your anus, as if you were stopping a fart, and by squeezing your urethra, as if you were stopping a stream of urine. If it's too taxing to squeeze them both simultaneously, choose one.

2. Now that you've located your pelvic floor, take a few deep breaths to center and relax.

3. Then, on an inhale, lift the pelvic floor. In other words, repeat Step 1, and hold your breath as you lift and hold for 3 seconds. (Build up to holding for 10 seconds.)

4. Exhale completely as you release.

5. Relax the pelvic floor muscles fully. Let it all go. Take a normal inhale and exhale.

6. Repeat steps 3, 4, and 5 at least three times.

⭐ Optional Visualization ⭐

Kundalini energy lies dormant at the base of the spine until it awakens. This energy is often described using the metaphor of a snake. If snakes turn you off in any way, replace the word "snake" with "wave of energy" in the following visualization.

Imagine a coiled snake that rests at the base of your spine begin to unfurl with each P-Pump. See/sense/feel the snake sensuously move up your spine at the back of your body. Feel it move up your neck and the back of your head. Then, see/sense/feel it slide over the top of your head and sensuously move down the front body. Repeat as many times as you'd like. Perhaps coordinate the visualization with the breath: the snake rising up the spine during an inhale and descending down the front body during an exhale.

Or the snakelike energy may just move upwards. The energy may pool along the way in various places in your body—the belly, the solar plexus, the heart, the throat, the third eye. Continue to lift, hold, and release the pelvic floor, doing as many P-Pumps as feels good. Notice the sensations in your body. Again, there is no right or wrong way to do this. Lean into what is most pleasurable for *you*.

Since the pelvic floor is made up of muscles, just like any muscle, it benefits from strengthening (i.e., P-Pumps) and from stretching. To stretch the pelvic floor, try a low, sustained squat or the yoga posture child's pose. While in either position, take slow, deep breaths and imagine your pelvic floor softening, opening, and releasing. P-Pumps are a phenomenal practice to use throughout the day to bring ourselves out of our heads and into our bodies.

Thoughts are what provoke feelings of shame and inadequacy. P-Pumps are a simple way to turn our attention toward pleasure and away from habitual, disempowering thoughts. The more we practice P-Pumps, the easier it is to bring ourselves pleasurably into this moment, *now*.

On the following journal page, write and/or draw what you noticed when you did some P-Pumps.

When I do P-Pumps,
I notice and feel...

Intentional Handshake

"When we're awake in our bodies and sense, the world comes alive. Wisdom, creativity, and love are discovered as we relax and awaken through our bodies."
—Tara Brach

Social norms have us extend a hand for a handshake when we first meet someone. What if the handshake was done with the same attention and intention as described in Exercise #4, where you bring your full awareness to the touch and open to pleasure?

♡ Challenge

Seek out an opportunity to shake someone's hand, or otherwise casually touch someone with consent. As you make physical contact, bring your attention to the sensation in your hand and observe what happens.

♡ Challenge Afterglow

How was that handshake different? How did a focus on the physical sensations affect your connection with yourself? With the other person?

Love Ripple Challenge Notes

Chapter 5
Self-Empowerment from the Inside Out

Sexual empowerment blooms from self-empowerment.

Just like there are many trails to the top when climbing a mountain, there are many ways to cultivate self-empowerment. One of the most potent paths I've found is to identify and get to know the characters that make up my inner pantheon.

⭐ Inner Pantheon? ⭐

Your inner pantheon is composed of the diverse aspects that make you you—your personality, your ego, and even your spirit. Just as the Greek or Roman gods symbolized different elements of the human experience, this is the personalized pantheon of your inner world. One way to identify characters in your inner pantheon is by discerning the various voices in your head. Another way to excavate these characters is to notice any strong reactions you have to people and specific life circumstances.

Take this playbook, for example. Have you noticed any voices in your head as you've been reading it? Any detractors saying, "Oh my, I couldn't possibly do something like that." Or maybe cheerleaders: "Oh yes! I've been waiting for something like this." Or perhaps shame-based thoughts like, "What would people think if I did this?" Or: "People will think I'm a total slut."

Capture any voices you've noticed in words or images in the following journal page. And, as you notice other voices, come back to the journal page and add them.

Voices in my head are saying...

In 2002, after reading Barbara Marx Hubbard's *Emergence: Shifting from Ego to Essence*, I began to identify and name the parts of my ego. As soon as an aspect of my personality had a name, I could engage with it more easily.

Penelope the Perfectionist Planner was the first in my inner pantheon to be named. Penelope had been instrumental in my academic and corporate success. Soon after Penelope got her name, I had a dream. A woman with glasses, short curly hair, and a great ass was standing at a large copy machine making copies. She was absorbed in the task and stood there for what seemed like hours. When I woke up, I remembered the dream and told Bill about it. As I described the woman at the copy machine, it dawned on me—that was Penelope!

✧ The Consciousness Roundtable ✧

Marta Maria Marraccini created another useful metaphor for understanding our inner lives: the consciousness roundtable. Imagine the parts of your personality all sitting around a large wooden table—just like King Arthur's Knights of the Round Table. In the middle of the table, there's a microphone. Only one. This means only one part of your ego can speak at any given time.

And so a game ensues. And this game is called: *Who has the mic?*
The objective is twofold:

1. Be able to identify who has the mic in any moment, and

2. Determine if that's the most sensible character in your inner pantheon to be holding the mic right now. If it's not, pass the mic to someone else.

I encourage you to try it for yourself. And remember: this is a game, an aspiration, an intention. The more you play, the better you'll get at knowing who has the mic—and the more seamlessly you'll be able to hand the mic to a character better-suited to the circumstance. For instance, when I'm organizing a fundraising event, Penelope is often the best one to have the mic. However, if I'm parenting, not so much. I may notice my child's resistance to a plan or strategy I suggested. Oftentimes, that tips me off—Penelope has the mic. And it may not be hers to hold right now. Because she can be overbearing and nitpicky, Penelope is usually not the right character to be playing the role of parent.

As you identify, name, and get to know the characters in your inner pantheon, you'll cultivate the ability to recognize who has the mic in any given moment. And this gives you the power to switch it up, if that's what's needed. It's so liberating (and playful!) to navigate the psyche in this way.

And somewhere along this road, inevitably you will meet your inner child.

 Embracing the Inner Child

One thing is indisputable: in every inner pantheon, at every consciousness round-table, there sits an inner child. And if we don't tend to this part, that child will find ways to sabotage our deepest desires.

Let me tell you a story.

A community meeting was called to discuss the growing number of unhoused residents living at a nearby park. Local elected officials and a few city employees led the meeting. After their brief presentation, each of the 200 people in attendance could make a public comment of up to one minute in length. I made my comment and left the meeting shortly after.

Hours later, I noticed my mind spinning. "If I'd only said this instead." "How could I have not said that?" "Why didn't I use my phone to track the time, since there wasn't a timer displayed?" And on and on.

In the middle of the night, still obsessing, I came up with the perfect comment. If only I'd thought of that yesterday, I fretted to myself. All of a sudden, a beam of clarity shone through: I could play *Who has the mic?*

I took some deep breaths and tried to settle myself. In my mind's eye, I saw her. It was eight-year-old Rachel who had the mic. She was clad in overalls wearing a headset microphone, since her hands were busy laying bricks. Rachel is one of my "protectors" who jumps in to defend me from the emotional pain of my inner child. She was writhing with regret, trying desperately to distract me from feeling like a failure, like I was worthless.

And right now, she was frantic. Attempting to build a buffer so I wouldn't feel my core wound. Her strategy was to occupy my mind with thoughts of how it *could* have gone in the hopes that somehow she could change the past. Or at least have me believe I was capable of doing better. But of course, Rachel's efforts were futile. Even knowing the perfect thing to say, the fact remained that I hadn't said it.

With Rachel on red alert, I knew my inner kid was close. So I turned my attention to Fanny.

Fanny is a harrowed-looking bird of a girl, maybe four years old, dressed in random bits and pieces gathered from free boxes. She wants nothing more than to be loved.

But in this moment, Fanny thought she had let me down—again. She felt like a failure. In my mind's eye, I invited her into my lap, where I held and rocked her. I whispered in her ear that I loved her, and we cuddled. Until my heartbeat slowed, my breathing deepened, and eventually I relaxed into sleep.

⭐ Core Wound: Always a Lie ⭐

Fanny is my inner wounded child. She came to be when I was just beginning to walk, at about one year old. Every time I managed to get my balance, my big brother— older by 22 months—would push me down. After this happened repeatedly, I simply stopped trying. That's when Fanny the Failure was born in my inner pantheon.

Eventually, I learned to walk, of course, but Fanny stuck around. Fanny believes I just don't matter. Soon after Fanny came to be, Rachel arrived as a survival mechanism to shield me from harm. Rachel's job has been to try to protect me from feeling this core wound of worthlessness. And she is deeply dedicated to that task.

Each of us has a core wound, stemming from something painful experienced at a young age. And from this wound, a core belief emerges. Such as: *I'm worthless. Nobody wants me. I can't trust anyone. I'm unlovable. I'm wrong.* Or some version of this. The beliefs accompanying our core wounds are almost always black-and-white, stripped of nuance—because in early childhood, our brains aren't developmentally capable of it.

Here's what's key to remember: Everyone's core belief is a lie. All core beliefs involve some version of our unlovableness and how we're wrong. And they simply are not true.

You'll have your own flavor of core belief, or what I call your *wounded kid mantra.* To discover or clarify your personal version of this, please take yourself on the guided journey below. This type of internal adventure is most meaningful when the conscious mind is relaxed, so you can let the subconscious lead in a semi-dreamlike state. To surrender into this experience, you have options: you can have a friend guide you through the journey, you can record it on your phone and play it back, or you can read it through a couple of times and practice from memory.

Also, this is a journey you may wish to take more than once, and even many times.

♡ GUIDED VISUALIZATION ♡

Visit with the Inner Child to Reveal Your Core Belief[13]

- Make sure you are in a comfortable position. You may want to lie down.

- Please use the 4-1-5 breath (as described in Exercise #1 on page 6), using the breath as a presencing tool (Exercise #6 on page 59), or a practice of your own to relax fully into this moment. Feel the support of the earth underneath you and let go further.

- Allow your awareness to drop into your heart or your belly. After a few deep breaths…

- You find yourself in a beautiful forest. Inhale the scent of pine and bay trees. You see a giant redwood at the far end of an open expanse of leaf-covered ground. You walk toward the massive tree, enjoying the soft buoyancy of leaves beneath your feet and the vast canopy of branches above. Right by the trunk of the tree you see a large hole. Curious, you peer into the darkness. It's vast. You lean in a little further and find yourself falling.

- Instead of fear, you feel a kind of freedom as you fall. You surrender to it fully, and spiral gracefully down, down, down. Eventually, you land gentle as a feather on a soft bed of leaves.

- Above you, you notice an otherworldly being hovering, a spirit guide or mythic creature. Who is it? Notice the details, their shape, the colors, their eyes.

- This being asks if you'd like to go on a trip into your childhood.

- If your answer is no, please don't worry. You may just not be quite ready to take this trip yet. Instead, let yourself rest in this place for as long as feels right. You and your guide fly back to the redwood tree. When you feel ready, gently open your eyes to come out of the meditation.

- If your answer is yes, let your guide take your hand. You begin rising together, up out of the hole, up above the treetops, until you're high in the sky. Together you fly over the forest, over mountains, over cities. Until finally you come to the outskirts of a city you recognize. It is the city in which you spent your childhood. A minute later, you're hovering above the neighborhood where you grew up.

- The next thing you know, you're inside your childhood home. Notice the sounds and smells. You look around and see a child in a nearby room. What is the child doing? How does the child look? How is the child holding their body? What is the child feeling? Observe whatever you can about this child.

- Then you recognize your childhood room—and that this child is *you*. As you gaze at your young self, you realize that you are embodying the Great Mother. The part of you that knows how to nurture, how to love unconditionally, and how to offer sanctuary to those in pain.

- You ask the child if you may speak with them. Allow the child to answer. If they say yes, ask if the child would like to sit on your lap. If they say no, ask if you can sit somewhere close by. If they aren't ready, go wherever they're comfortable having you. Notice what, if anything, the child seems to be afraid of.

- If the child is warming to you, trusting you, and perhaps even sitting on your lap, ask the child to recall an experience when they felt most hurt. As the nurturing parent, take care to provide any comfort or support that will help the child feel safe to remember such things. Continue holding the child until they share the deep wound. Please don't force the child to share or take it personally if they don't share. Trust must be cultivated. If the child chooses not to tell you about the core wound, your job is to simply love them until they feel safe enough to share. Which means you may need to journey back again and again.

- When the child tells you about the deep hurt, ask the child what they decided about themselves and began to believe about themselves because of this experience. "This means that I am ________." Allow the child to speak about what they made up about themselves. Listen closely for the belief system that was constructed out of this core wound. (You may notice how this belief system connects to times when your adult self reacts out of seemingly nowhere.)

- When they're finished speaking, gently ask your inner child: What were you most afraid of in that moment? What did you want to ask for? What was the message you, the child, most wanted to hear from the person who hurt you?

- Listen closely to the message your inner child has to share.

- Then say the words the child most longed to hear back to the child. Or, if it's not clear, say whatever feels most authentic. Here is some of what I say to my inner kid: "I will never leave you. I will never criticize, reject, or hurt you. I am here for you. You are so precious to me. No matter what has happened in the past, I love you unconditionally. You are safe with me. I will listen to you. I will come back and visit you. I love you."

- Allow an image or symbol to arise that is a metaphor for your connection with your inner child. Tell your inner child that you will use this symbol or image to connect with them on the inner planes, in dreamtime, and whenever is needed.

- Then lovingly set them down and say goodbye in whatever way feels right to you. Let your inner kid know that they're not alone—that you will be returning to check in with them. Because just as in any relationship, you must build trust with this sensitive, vulnerable part of yourself. Reassure them that you'll be back, and that you care very deeply for them.

- When you're ready, you exit the door of the home you grew up in with your guide. You both fly up into the sky, through the darkness of the void, and back up into the trunk of the tree. When you are ready, you step out of the tree into the magical forest.

- You know you can return to this forest and this tree any time you wish to visit your inner child.

- Slowly shift your awareness to your breathing. Take as much time as you'd like to follow the breath. When you're ready, begin to let a little light into your eyes and bring yourself back.

Make notes or sketches in the following journal page about your encounter with your inner child. Did you discover your core belief/wounded kid mantra?

Please be patient with this precious part of you. Many of our inner kids have been cast aside and ignored for a long time. They often reside in a deep, dark place on the outskirts of our awareness. It is totally natural to encounter challenging emotions as you open to your inner wounded child. Keep evoking the Great Mother part of you, and don't give up on your inner kid.

Connecting with my inner child

Once you've established a connection, you may wish to have a nightly ritual of tucking them in or greeting the morning together. It can be fun to draw your inner kid out by asking them questions. For example: *What do you want to wear today? What would you like for breakfast? What's your favorite treat? When do you have the most fun?* Listen to their answers, and I encourage you to indulge and play with them.

And, music may be a helpful balm. I remember listening to Shaina Noll's song *How Could Anyone* on repeat for hours holding myself in the fetal position, crying, releasing, and loving myself into wholeness. There may be a song that melts your and your inner kid's hearts together.

As you foster trust with your inner kid, your ability to handle challenging situations and emotions will grow. And your access to pleasure and sensuality will likely expand as well.

⭐ My Inner Pantheon ⭐

I encourage you to take on the practice of naming the characters in your inner pantheon. Or you can let them name themselves! They may come up with something you'd never dream of. Personally, naming the characters in my inner pantheon has made it easier for me to get to know them. And recently I had Donna Kiddie, a priestess sister, sketch some of them for this playbook. And wow, did that ever bring them to life!

Allow me, dear reader, to introduce you to more of my inner pantheon…

Entering stage left is my divine child, Little Elana. Distinct from the wounded inner child, each of us also has a divine child inside. This is the innocent, radiant, uniquely ingenious part of us—the one who knows they're whole and complete no matter what.

Somewhere in the background, and right there on the bottom left, is Disconnected D. She came to be when I was about five. She is masterful at becoming almost invisible and going to an imaginary refuge I call "the golden place." In a household with a lot of financial stress and passive aggression, plus an older sibling who consumed almost all parental attention, disassociating was an emotional survival tactic. Since D had no idea what she wanted, she often took center stage in my adolescence and young adulthood, when I strove to do what others wanted in order to win their approval.

As you practice a Sure Thing, you will certainly become more intimate with the part of you that revels in pleasure. You may call this part your inner slut or gigolo, or your inner love god or goddess, or perhaps something else entirely—your inner erotic creature, your wild sensual self, your inner lover, or another name that turns you on.

⭐ My Wild Sensual Self ⭐

Vivacious Viv is my wild sensual self, and she is thrilled to meet you. Viv has a huge appetite for sex and physical arousal, and a passion for all embodied experience. She loves taking huge bites out of life—and also certain bare necklines! Viv came out during brief sexual encounters in my teens and early twenties but otherwise was hidden away. Given I was raised to be a "good girl," Viv didn't get much access to the mic. That is, until she made an explosive entrée in my early thirties, when I left my marriage and dove headfirst into a world of sensuality and sex.

Clarissa Pinkola Estes, a Jungian psychoanalyst and author of *Women Who Run with the Wolves,* writes: "Overkill through excesses, or excessive behaviors is acted out by women who are famished for a life that has meaning and makes sense for them."[14]

Alcohol, drugs, rage, promiscuity, overeating, obsessive fitness, and dieting—all of these can be overkill through excess. I tended toward overeating and obsessive fitness, and for good reason. Having Disconnected D come on the scene at an early age, I found ways, though sometimes harmful, to get me into my body to feel something, anything.

I was myself famished for a life of meaning. That's when I first really came to know Viv. For decades I had repressed her, and now she wanted the mic all the time. That's often the case when an aspect of self that hasn't gotten much airtime is finally given permission to take center stage. At first, I did overdo it. I joined a cult focused on female orgasm and turned away from most everything else in my life, including loved ones. Thankfully, that only lasted eight months.

Over the years, Viv has inspired me to do things I never thought I could, like running for city council and starting a global love experiment. And The Sure Thing was most definitely her brainchild. Even though my wild self barged into my consciousness decades before the invention of The Sure Thing, this part didn't have a name. Without a name, she was still an amorphous aspect of my personality.

A few months after we started our Sure Thing practice, I took note of the creative vixen who came out each week to guide us into uncharted territory. That's when Vivacious Viv got her name. Once, as Bill washed his hands in the bathroom and

I lounged in our bed, Viv reached into the jar of lube on the nightstand and boldly started stroking my clit. When he came into the bedroom, Viv told him to take off his pants. Now mutual masturbation is a gratifying option in our ever-growing palette of Sure Thing possibilities—all thanks to Viv!

She enters other arenas of my life, too. I have Viv to thank for learning to ski at the age of 54—it was her appetite for adventure that gave me the courage. She also led me to the dojo, where I discovered a passion for Aikido and am on track to becoming a black belt by the age of 60. Of course, there were many instances in my life when Viv tried to get my attention, but I ignored her. For example, when my first husband proposed: a volcano of dread erupted in my belly, which I now know was Viv screaming "NO!"

I've come to learn that Viv mainly hangs out in my womb and pussy. Knowing that, when I have an important choice to make, or otherwise notice a strong sensation there, I pause and check in with her. It matters to me that she's on board, because then I know whatever it is will really be right for me.

Growing up in a sexually repressive culture, you may have marginalized your wild sensual self. Or perhaps your early childhood environment pushed you into dissociation. Or there may have been a particular incident—traumatic or otherwise—that caused you to shun your wild self. Or perhaps you, like me, were the "good" child, which left no space in your psyche for your wild self to thrive.

If you have yet to befriend your wild self, you may feel some resistance at first to even considering a Sure Thing practice. You may have judgments, such as: "I don't need this" or "What a waste of time." Be honest with yourself. Don't override these thoughts and push forward—that won't support your Sure Thing practice or your attainment of self-empowerment. In fact, it may have the opposite effect and undermine your efforts. Instead, I encourage you to look at these judgments, so you can open to this potent, and sometimes intimidating, part of you. We need to bring everyone inside us, all of those in our inner pantheon, along for the ride. Otherwise, we won't reach our destination of deeper fulfillment and fuller sexual expression.

So, what to do?

Make a different choice and start a new pattern: observe these judgments without believing them—and then go befriend your wild self! Tune into this part of you. Invite it to reveal itself. Don't coerce, simply let this part know you want to get to know it better.

The guided visualization below is designed to help you connect with your wild sensual self. This type of internal adventure is most meaningful when the conscious mind is relaxed, so you can let the subconscious lead in a semi-dreamlike state. To surrender into this experience, you have options: you can have a friend guide you through the journey, you can record it on your phone and play it back, or you can read it through a couple of times and practice from memory.

Note: I've used feminine pronouns in this exercise. Please change the pronouns to suit you.

 GUIDED VISUALIZATION~HELLO Wild Sensual Self!

Start by centering yourself, and clearing your heart and head. You may use one of the grounding exercises from a previous chapter or a practice of your own.

- Imagine your consciousness is like an anchor. See, feel, sense your attention dropping from your head to your heart, and then to your belly. Take a few deep breaths.

- Allow a time to come to mind when you felt a tingle in your genitals. You felt turned on and sexually aroused. Maybe there was an object of your desire—a crush, chemistry with a lover or someone you just met, or even some creative inspiration that got your juices flowing. Pheromones were flaming, maybe there was some flushing. A moment you felt alive and filled with desire.

- From the tingle in your genitals, allow yourself to open and connect with the aspect of your inner pantheon associated with sexual pleasure. Home into that memory with as much vividness as possible. What were your thoughts? What were the other sensations in your body? Observe the moment in as much detail as you can. What did you ask for? What might you have wanted to ask for, but didn't?

- Now allow another experience to arise, another moment when you felt aroused, turned on, and sexually activated. As above, see it in detail.

- Next, invite connections to start to develop between these experiences. What sensations were similar? What desires? What felt heightened in your mind and body?

- Now see if you can locate the home of your wild sensual self. Does she lounge in a luxurious temple, amid pink pillows, satin sheets, and rose petals? Or maybe she reclines in a hot tub under a starry sky. Or perhaps she's lying on a chaise in a boudoir filled with plates of delicacies, bouquets of flowers, and sensual playmates responding to her every whim. Or maybe she's just waking up now on a deserted beach, stretching out her legs so the waves reach them. Wherever she is, see if you can locate her in your body and your mind.

- Now notice how your wild sensual self responds to your attention. Is she receptive, softening, opening? If not, ask her what she needs to feel more comfortable. Certain words? A hug? An assurance of safety or privacy? Whatever it is, give it to her.

- Once you sense her relaxing, ask her to show you how she has been with you over the years. Allow visions, sensations, and memories from throughout your life to surface. When was she fully expressed, seen, received? Even if they were rare, even if it was decades ago, let these moments flood your heart, body, and mind. These were instances when she was holding the mic.

- Now, ask your wild sensual self to show you examples of when she was silenced or ignored. Maybe she was trying to make herself known through sensations in your body—a sense of emptiness in the belly, a tightening in the chest, a closing of the yoni. Allow yourself to receive any images, memories, or feelings from moments she tried to communicate with you but couldn't get through.

- Make any amends you feel are authentic. The Ho'oponopono prayer—"I'm sorry. Please forgive me. Thank you. I love you"—can be a beautiful practice to use here, if it feels resonant.

- Next, ask her if there's anything else she would like to tell you. And let her know how you feel about being connected with her in this way.

- Ask her what her name is.

- Finally, as in any relationship, you must build trust with this part of self. Let her know when you'll be coming back to check in on her—and be sure to show up!

- When you're ready, bid farewell to your wild sensual self. Take as much time as you'd like to follow the breath. Perhaps place one hand on your heart and the other on your belly. When you're ready, begin to let a little light into your eyes and bring yourself back.

Make notes or sketches in the journal page below about your encounter with your wild self.

⭐ Cultivate a Relationship with Your Wild Self ⭐

I encourage you to make a practice of listening to your wild self. Ask them questions, such as: *What do you desire? What turns you on? Where do you feel the most expressed? How do you like to play? What do you want? How would you like to spend the next hour, or even the next ten minutes?*

Pamper this erotic part of you! Let them have the mic, and even, at times, be the MC of your life story. As with any relationship, devote time, energy, and attention to get to know this part of yourself. Know that there are infinite ways to deepen your intimacy with your wild, sensuous nature.

⭐ Your Inner Pantheon ⭐

As you begin a Sure Thing practice, you may get to know aspects of yourself you hadn't encountered before. In the scroll below, identify some of the characters in your inner pantheon. Which are the parts of your personality that you can easily identify? The "Voices in my head are saying" journal page in this chapter may be a good resource. List the parts of your inner pantheon in the following scroll, including your wild self and your inner kid.

Add to this list as you uncover more of the players in your inner pantheon.

Self-empowerment grows when we know ourselves, acknowledge our gifts, and recognize our limitations and growing edges. The more we befriend ourselves, the more authentic we are—and the more fulfilling life becomes! Inner knowing elicits self-confidence, forthrightness, and dignity. Not only will a Sure Thing practice expand your capacity for pleasure, it will also awaken sovereignty, self-love, and authenticity. In short: when you practice The Sure Thing, you are actively practicing self-empowerment.

Share Your Inner Pantheon

"To love oneself is the beginning of a lifelong romance."
—Oscar Wilde

Being truly known by another begins with a willingness to share ourselves vulnerably, especially the parts we may judge.

♥ Challenge

Introduce a character from your inner pantheon to a loved one in a nonjudgmental and playful way. Extra credit: Invite your friend or family member to call this character by name, should they notice that they have the mic. I suggest you choose a loved one you sense will be receptive to this kind of exercise, at least the first time.

♥ Challenge Afterglow

Did the level of connection and intimacy change when you shared about your inner pantheon? If yes, how? How did the character in your inner pantheon respond to being introduced?

Love Ripple Challenge Notes

Chapter 6
Learning to Ask for What You Want

One of the keys to manifesting your dreams is making bold requests.

I knew what I wanted. And I knew I had to tell him immediately. I'd just completed a day-long medicine journey with my Hakomi therapist, and I could no longer live in denial. But I was terrified. My knuckles were white on the steering wheel as I drove home.

My husband was sitting in the den on the blue-and-white-striped loveseat. I walked into the room, stood in front of him, and said, "I want to end our marriage."

I watched as he sobbed into his hands, torn, knowing I could make it all better. Part of me yearned to sit next to him and take it back. Stuff down what I knew was right for me and go along with what he wanted. But the truth is I never wanted to be married to this man. I just hadn't had the courage to say no when he proposed years earlier. And now, finally, I'd summoned it.

My heart was breaking, too, watching him. It was a very difficult moment, and it is worth mentioning that when I ran into my ex a few years later, he was happily remarried with two young kids. My staying in that marriage ultimately wasn't serving either of us. But at the time, it took everything I had to witness his pain while staying connected to my own truth. Which streamed through my entire body—electric, alive, undeniable. For maybe the first time in my life, I had total clarity.

After that day, I realized that in order to stay connected to my truth, I had to check in with myself regularly. So I created a practice of asking myself throughout the day, "What do I want? What do I want to eat? What do I want to wear? What do I want to do?" Over and over and over again. I needed to build this muscle of self-discovery.

At first, my mind would be completely blank. Or the words "I don't know" would pop into my head. But as long as I was willing to ride out the initial frustration and practice patience, something would always arise. And as I continued to ask myself, "What do I want?" the answer came more easily. Just like muscle memory: the more you use it, the more access you develop.

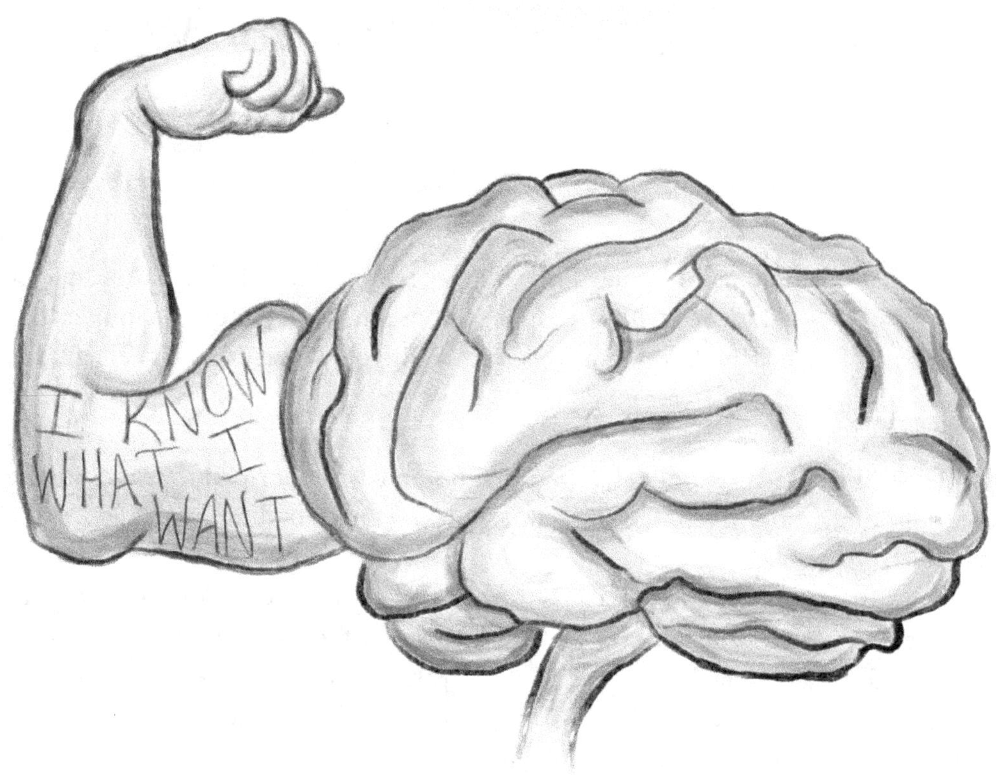

⭐ Knowing What You Want ⭐

You must know what you want before you can ask for it. Ask yourself: Can I easily access what it is I desire? Or is it difficult to figure out what I really want? Like me, you may have a character or two in your inner pantheon who wreak havoc with your "I know what I want" muscle.

First, we have Astrid the Accommodator, who thrives on the approval of others. She has the remarkable ability to bend like a willow branch, fluid and flexible. Astrid is an expert compromiser and even better capitulator. She loves nothing more than to win others' approval. Her logic is: If I go along with what you want, I will please you *and* I won't need to do the work to detect what it is that I want. She's especially effective when in cahoots with Disconnected D. That's my dissociated part. Astrid the Accommodator lays the groundwork, and then Disconnected D floats onto the scene and all I experience is a blurry disassociation.

If you have your own inner accommodator or pleaser or some other character who gets in the way of you knowing exactly what it is you want, try asking yourself throughout the day, "What do I want?" Even for the most inconsequential things. At your bathroom sink, "Do I want to wash my face or brush my teeth first?"

It may seem small, and sometimes it is. But the more you hone this muscle, the more you'll be able to perceive your genuine preferences.

⭐ The Body is a Messenger ⭐

The body is a phenomenal resource. If we tune in and pay attention, the body will usually provide the answer we are seeking. Sometimes our body's guidance is subtle, like a whisper. Other times, our body communicates loud and clear. Let's try an exercise...

💟 EXERCISE 8: Your Internal Guidance System 💟

Bring to mind a choice you need to make. It could be something as pedestrian as what you want to eat for dinner, or it could be a life-altering decision. Or anything in between.

1. Center yourself by inhaling "Open" and exhaling "Empty," or use another technique to quiet the mind and bring your full attention to this moment.

2. Once you feel settled, notice what happens in your body when you say "I'm going to _________ (insert one of your choices). If you'd like, say it out loud.

3. Pay attention to your body's response, including sensations, emotions, and feelings your body may provide.

4. Center yourself once again. Allow your thoughts to clear.

5. When you feel settled, notice what happens in your body when you say "I'm going to _________ (insert the *other* choice).

6. Pay attention to your body's response, including sensations, emotions, and feelings your body may provide.

7. What did you notice? Does this help clarify which choice is right for you?

This is a simple and amazingly effective tool. All you need to do is ask the question and listen for the physical response. The mind will spin a thousand tales… but the body never lies.

To sense if someone is right for you as a lover, adrienne maree brown's advice is spot on. That is, to be able to identify at least three different physical and emotional signals of a distinct yes. "Signs like quickening breath, flushed face, pressure in the groin, sweat on the palms, tingling up the spine, weakening in the knees, and so much more."[15] Once you know your "yes," then your "no" becomes clear, too.

Use the following journal page to track what it is you want throughout the day. If you don't get an immediate answer, be patient. Take a few deep breaths. Notice if you have bodily responses to your query. Use the space on the next page to track your answers. Even if it's "I don't know what I want," write that down. Continue this practice until you can regularly identify what it is you want.

What I want, what I really, really want!

Date/Time   <u>What do I want?</u>

____

____

____

____

____

____

____

____

____

____

____

____

☆ Ask for What You Want ☆

Once you know what you want, do you actually ask for it? For example, do you ask for a raise when you deserve it? Do you ask for more time with friends or family when you want it? This is where courage, self-love, and non-attachment are invited to join the party. Permit me to elaborate…

- **Courage:** When you ask for what you want, you put yourself out there and take a risk. It's intrinsically vulnerable—because the other person may meet us, or they may leave us hanging. Like reaching out a hand, we don't know if it'll be taken. But the only way to find out is to risk rejection and ask for what we want.

- **Self-Love:** If you are turned down, know that you are worthy of having this desire fulfilled, even if it doesn't happen immediately. Loving yourself and knowing that you are worthy *no matter what* is essential.

- **Non-attachment:** As we build our "asking for what we want" muscle, non-attachment is foundational. Of course this is easier said than done! But it's helpful to adopt a mindset of trust that you *will* fulfill your desires. It may not look exactly like you planned, though. Keep your attention on actualizing your desire, even if it requires asking for what you want many times, in various ways and/or from different people.

In the early months of strengthening my "asking for what I want" muscle, I had a super-hot yoga instructor. One morning during class, as he walked around the room making hands-on adjustments, I had a burning desire to ask him out. Nervous excitement flooded my body.

After class, I hung around in the lobby while he talked with other students. As he walked toward me, belly full of butterflies, I said, "I'm really attracted to you. Would you like to go out sometime?"

He smiled and said, "Thanks, I'm flattered, but I don't date my students." Even though I knew he had recently made out with another student, I didn't care. I didn't even feel rejected. I'd never asked anyone out before. It didn't matter that he said no. I was exhilarated that I asked for exactly what I wanted.

If you're someone who doesn't regularly ask for what you want, I challenge you to take a leap of faith. Discover something or someone that you desire. Then, love yourself up. Make sure that your inner kid is included and feels well-loved and tended to. Next, draw up all of your courage and *ask for what you want.*

If you receive a "no," notice what's happening in your mind and body. If you observe negative or critical self-talk, it's likely your inner kid is feeling rejected. Gather them up in a hug. I like to literally hug myself: wrap my arms around my chest and hold the opposite shoulder blade with my hands. You may want to rock yourself, too. Most importantly, let your inner kid know that you love them, that they are amazing, and that no matter what anyone else does or doesn't do, they are loved and valued by *you.*

"Song in My Soul" by Katie Berggren

Practice asking for what you want in different areas of your life and from a variety of people in your life. The more you practice, the more resilient you will become, and the easier it will be to ask for exactly what it is you want. Use the following tally sheet to support you in this exploration.

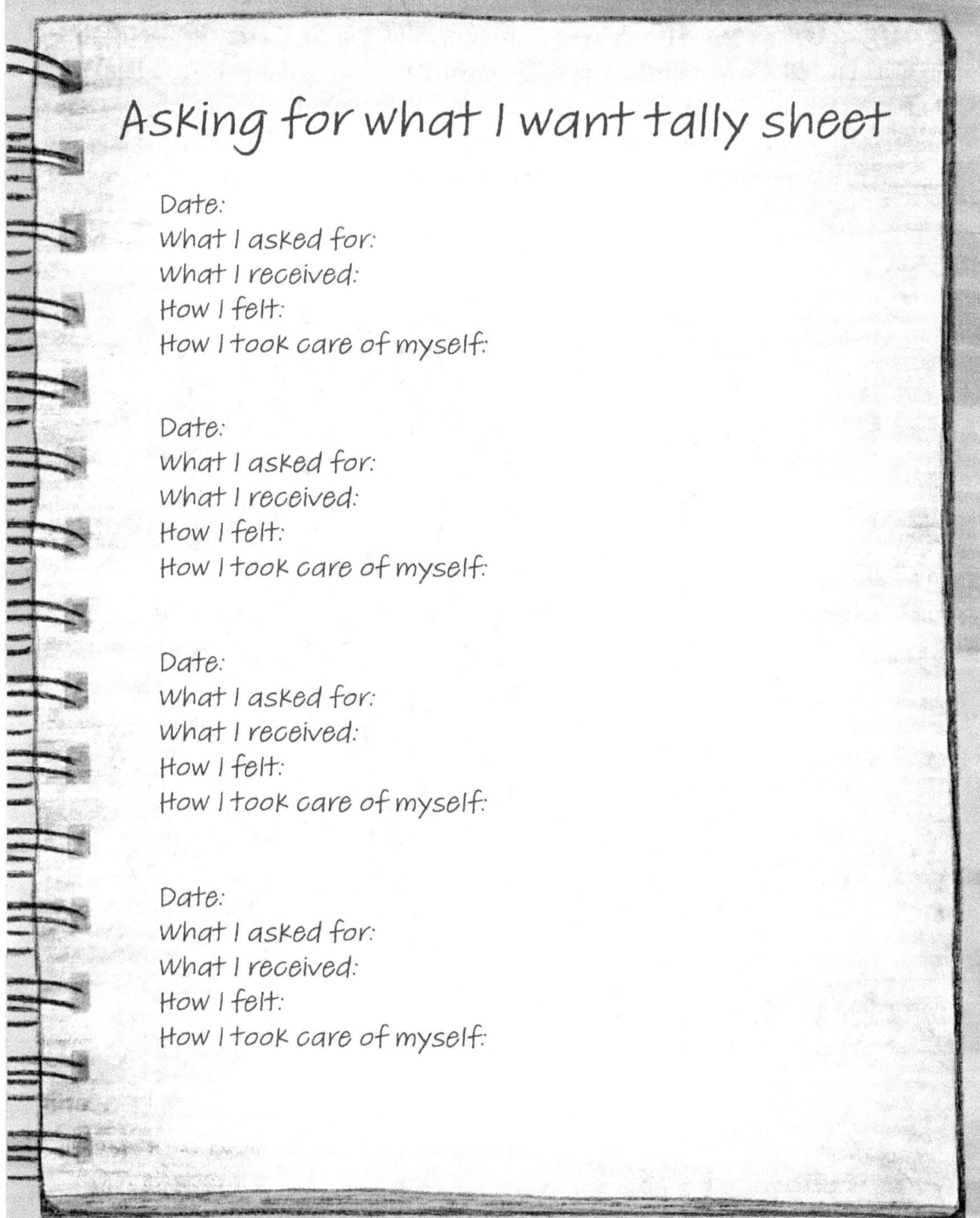

Asking for what I want tally sheet

Date:
What I asked for:
What I received:
How I felt:
How I took care of myself:

Date:
What I asked for:
What I received:
How I felt:
How I took care of myself:

Date:
What I asked for:
What I received:
How I felt:
How I took care of myself:

Date:
What I asked for:
What I received:
How I felt:
How I took care of myself:

⭐ Make a Request and Then... ⭐

During a recent Sure Thing, my beloved wanted to be inside of me. I checked in with my pussy and she said, "No, thank you." Then, I thought of his cock in my mouth. And I got excited.

"Instead of my pussy, I'll take you into my mouth," I counteroffered. Lying back, he nodded with a smile.

When we make a request or when someone makes a request of us, there are always three options: accept it, reject it, or counteroffer.

When someone makes a request of you, it's important to stay attuned to what is true for you. Overriding your internal guidance to please someone else is counterproductive to expanding your capacity to ask for what you want. Be true to yourself and your own desires. If you need time to consider a request, ask for it. Then, use whatever practice helps you connect with your more subtle inner knowing to guide you to an authentic response.

With a request,
you can...
✓ accept
✗ reject
• or counteroffer!

☆ Request vs. Demand ☆

Bring to mind a time when someone requested something from you. Really sink in and recall it fully—where were you, where was the other, what time of day was it etc. Then: How did it feel in your body? What did you notice about the person making the request? What happened afterward?

Now, bring to mind an instance when someone demanded something of you. And here, do the same—recall it in full detail. How did that feel? What did you notice about the person making the demand? What happened afterward? Jot down your thoughts, recollections, and reflections below.

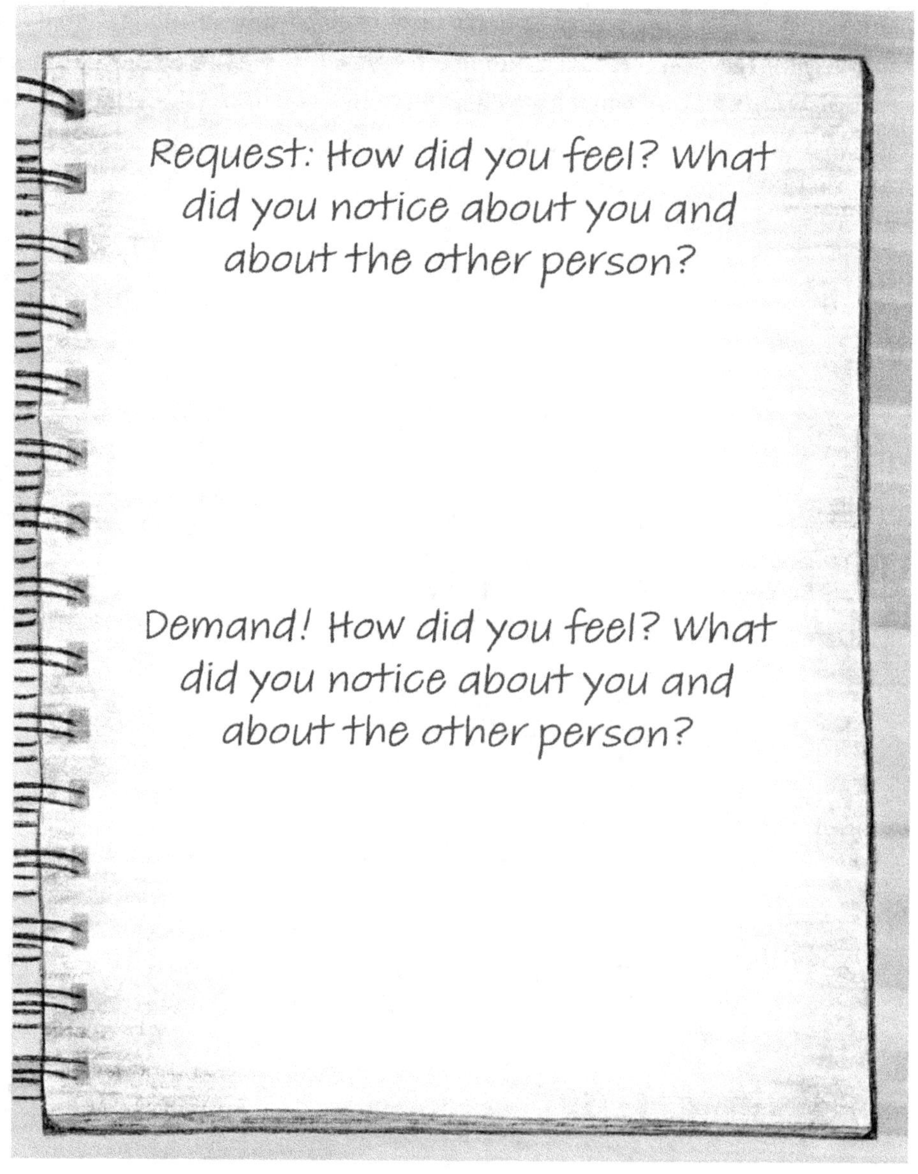

Personally, when someone requests something of me, I feel open to possibility and relaxed. But with a demand, I feel confined, even coerced. These physical reactions are helpful cues. I've learned to slow down and notice them, especially before responding to what feels like a demand.

Return to the request and demand you brought to mind. What do you notice about the other person's tone and body language in both circumstances?

⭐ Components of Communication ⭐

All verbal communication includes:

1. the actual words spoken,

2. the tone used, and

3. body language.

These three components will often reveal whether something is a request or a demand. For example, "Would you pass the salt?" could be delivered with a neutral tone and passive body language (i.e., arms relaxed at your sides). Or "Would you pass the salt?" could be spoken with an aggressive tone and confrontational body language (i.e., hands on hips). Using the same words, the first one would be received as a request, whereas the second one would likely be received as a demand.

When you intend to make a request of someone, I encourage you to first take a moment and soften. Drop your awareness into your belly and heart. Sometimes when I do this, I notice agitation or impatience. Then if I go ahead and make the request, it often doesn't go so well, as my tone tends to be harsh. Luckily for me, my spouse and son are always willing to point out that I sound severe or frustrated. And when that happens, I ask for a do-over. I take a deep breath and when I feel calmer, I try again.

Be gentle with yourself and one another as you traverse this tricky and nuanced world of communication. Give yourself and your beloveds the opportunity to try again and again and again until it feels right. Remember, this is a practice, not a perfection.

☆ Ready, Set, Ask! ☆

Now that we know what to expect when we make a request, how to take care of ourselves when we take a risk, and the basic components of communication, let's practice asking for what we want.

I recommend that you begin in the realm of the mundane. Let your beloved—a friend or family member you interact with regularly—know you're strengthening your "asking for what I want" muscle. Then, make requests. Ask if they would do the dishes, take out the trash, scratch your back, help you with _____ (fill in the blank with anything non-sensual/sexual).

Once you're warmed up and ready, begin to make requests in the sensual sphere. Let your intimate partner know you're building your "asking for what I want" muscle so they can be your ally as you cultivate this skill.

♥ EXERCISE 9: Asking for What I Want from a Lover ♥

First, read through the entire exercise a few times together. Then enact it from memory. Do the best you can to recall the specifics of the exercise, but don't focus on getting it exactly right. Allow yourself to surrender to your own inner knowing and guidance as you ask for what you want from a lover.

1. Take a deep breath and let your mind and energy settle into your belly.

2. Ask yourself, "What do I want right now?" Or "What would be most pleasurable?"

3. Listen for an answer that may come in words or an image.

4. Then ask your beloved for exactly that.

5. As you enjoy and surrender to how that feels, stay connected with yourself and your inner knowing. It takes some practice to open to sensation while simultaneously distinguishing if what is happening right now is satisfying or if you prefer something else. A key here is to take it slow.

6. Open to receive the full pleasure in the moment and allow your beloved to take you on a ride.

7. If at some point you can't surrender, it may be because you want something else. Ask your beloved to hold still so you can better perceive what it is you want.

8. Return to Step 1. Repeat as often as you desire.

⛧ Gamify Making Requests of a Lover ⛧

Set a timer for 3 minutes or more. During that time, continuously make requests for what you want. Begin by attuning to your body. Then, ask for something you would like your partner to do. After relaxing into that for a bit, actively turn your attention to what else you want. Then ask for it. As completely as you can, revel in the experience and then ask for something else. Continue this pattern until the timer goes off. Then, switch. Now it's your partner's turn to make requests.

Notice what's easier for you—being the giver or being the receiver.

Afterwards, I invite you to take some time to reflect: How do you react when your beloved makes requests? Do you feel criticized? Do you feel thankful for the guidance? Do requests make you feel more open or more closed? What would make you more receptive to your beloved's request? Would you like more acknowledgment?

Make some notes about what you're learning on the following journal page.

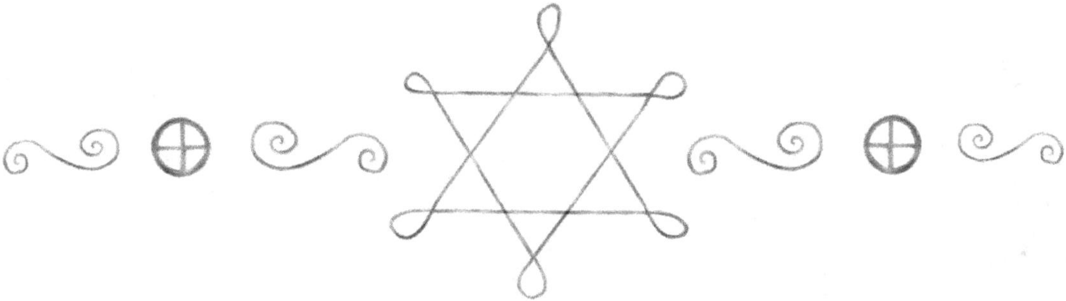

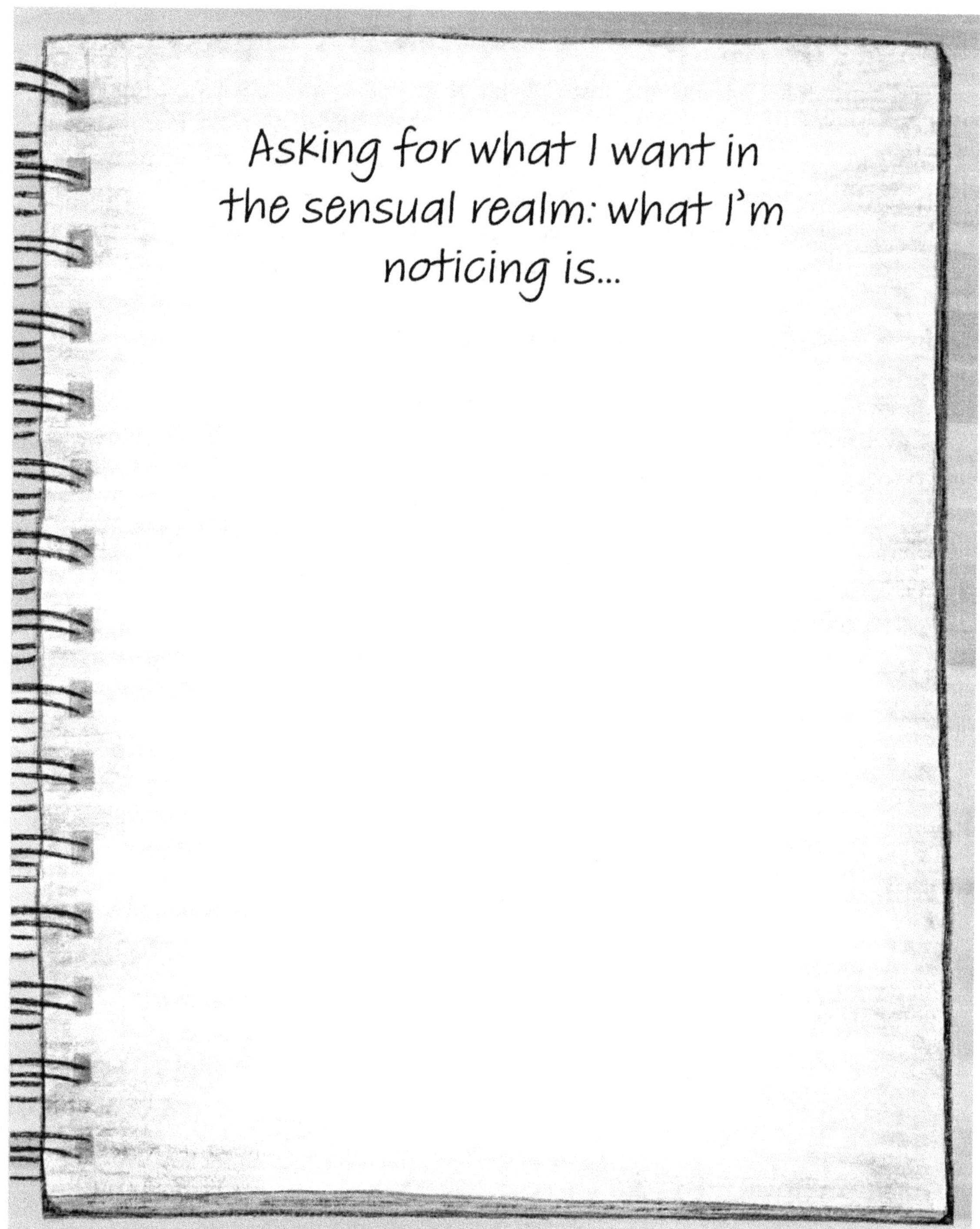
Asking for what I want in
the sensual realm: what I'm
noticing is...

Know that we each have different ways of communicating, both in the way we make requests as well as in how we like to be asked. Get to know your own style and your beloved's style. Share with each other what you're learning about yourself. Be curious. Ask each other questions. Not only will this strengthen your ability to ask for what you want, it will engender more intimacy in your relationship.

And let it be playful! Let it be fun, an unfolding adventure. I encourage you to invent your own games and experiments to practice this life-altering skill of asking for what you want.

♥ EXERCISE 10: Sensual Fulfillment Formula ♥

To ensure my sensual fulfillment, I've come up with this formula:

1. Attune to my body, drop into my belly (aka cauldron of desire) and ask myself, "What do I most want now?"

2. Open to receive a thought or an image of something that turns me on.

3. Ask my beloved for exactly what I want, as specifically as possible.

4. Acknowledge my beloved for whatever he is doing.

5. Repeat if I find my mind wandering and/or if I desire something else.

Here's how my sensual fulfillment formula may play out:
"Lover, please kiss and nibble on the back of my neck," I might say. When he obliges, I let the tingles from his scratchy beard kisses roll through my body. Then I realize I want a softer bite. "Please," I say, "gentler nibbles. Oh yes, that's it."

Then I might get an image of him with my nipples between his teeth. "Now, would you take off my shirt and nibble on my nipples?"

"Oh, that's nice! Would you bite a little harder? Wait, that's a little too hard. Ah… that's better." I let the pleasure saturate my breasts, spread out into my heart and chest, and ripple out through my entire body. After a bit, I might notice my clitoris is engorged and begging for a little attention.

"Lover, would you gently lick my clitoris?" I'll say. Or "Lover, would you remove my pants, get some lube, and stroke my clit?"

Then: "That feels so good. I feel energy running down my legs. Would you stroke a little lighter/firmer? That's so good. Would you stroke faster/slower?"

And on it goes. I try to feel each and every stroke. I can always ask my lover to pause to give me a chance to open more or to discern what I want now. There is no rush and nowhere to get to. It's about being right here, right now—all with the intention of relaxing into pleasure.

I invite you to uncover your own sensual fulfillment formula. You can take my sensual fulfillment formula for a test ride and see if it fits. Or you may want to make some tweaks or invent your own entirely.

When you know the steps in a progression that dependably brings you sensual fulfillment, enter them in the scroll below.

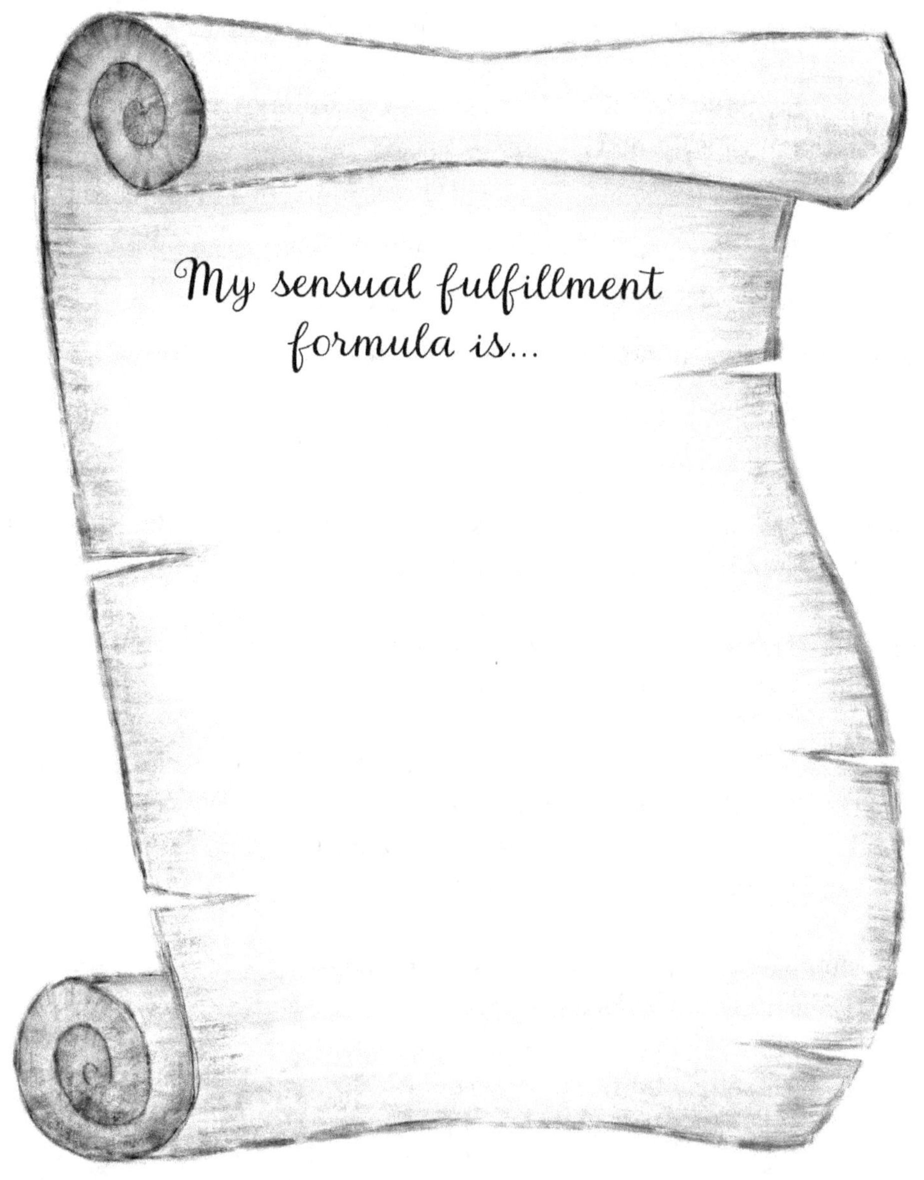

Keep in mind that the objective of the Sure Thing is to stay connected with yourself and your beloved no matter what. If you're doing a Solo Sure, you are your own beloved. If you start to feel resentful or less connected with yourself and/or your beloved, PAUSE. This itself can feel like a risky thing to do—will I lose my turn-on? Will I lose connection with my lover? But trust me when I tell you it'll pay off. You get to call a timeout so you can re-center yourself, clear the slate, and start again. To tune in to what you want now. And then ask for it.

Our desires are continuously changing, ebbing, and flowing. The best way I've found to navigate this ever-changing landscape is to ask myself often, "What do I want now?" And this is true whether lounging in bed with my partner or studying the menu at a taqueria.

Remember, the more you ask for what you want, the easier it will get. And the more you will build that muscle of attuning to the nuances of your changing appetite.

Inviting a Partner to Practice a Sure Thing

If you're clear you want to practice the Sure Thing with a partner and you know who that partner is, here's your invitation. Be certain you are both in a heart-centered, relaxed, and receptive place. Make it clear this is a special practice. And if it resonates, do what I did and invite your beloved in the postcoital afterglow.

If you get turned down, don't get discouraged. Don't take it personally. The practice may be intimidating to your partner, or there could be some other reason they aren't a yes. Be curious.

If they say no, ask if they're willing to have a conversation about it. And if they are, ask what it is about a Sure Thing they're not interested in. Listen with an open heart and mind. Be patient as you work your way to a place of mutual understanding. Then, create a roadmap for where you want to go. You may be headed in the same direction, and you may not. In the meantime, consider starting a Solo Sure practice.

Feed the Feminine First

"Today, like every other day, we wake up empty and frightened. Don't open the door to the study and begin reading. Take down a musical instrument. Let the beauty we love be what we do. There are hundreds of ways to kneel and kiss the ground."

—Rumi

♥ Challenge

When you first wake up in the morning, choose to do something that nourishes you. This may mean you get up a bit earlier than usual so you have time to ask yourself, "What would be most nurturing for me right now? How do I most want to pamper and tend to myself?"

Perhaps it's a bath, some yoga, meditation, a walk in the woods, snuggling with a hot cup of tea or a pet, journaling, writing poetry, making art, making music, dancing, or pleasuring yourself.

♥ Challenge Afterglow

How did you feed the feminine first today? What effect did it have on you? On the rest of your day?

Love Ripple Challenge Notes

Chapter 7
The Solo Sure: More in Love with ME

When you love yourself, you bless everyone around you.

I waited until I had a willing partner to begin this weekly practice, but there's absolutely no need to wait for anyone. Rather than putting things off until Prince or Princess Charming arrives on the scene, start with a Solo Sure. That's right, *you* take charge of your sensual and sexual fulfillment.

Remember from Chapter 1, you are 100% responsible for your pleasure. It's true, you have the keys to your temple of ecstasy. Because of that, even if you have a partner, I encourage you to read this chapter and fall more in love with you. And for those occasions when your partner isn't around.

⭐ Inner Lover ⭐

A Solo Sure is a self-love practice. And what better way to start than to acquaint yourself with your inner lover. Your inner lover is that part of you that's randy, that gets turned on, that's lusty, that shows up in the bedroom, that loves love, flirtation, pleasure, and sensuality in all of its forms. You may find that your inner lover *is* your wild sensual self, who you got to know in Chapter 5. Or you may uncover another aspect of your inner pantheon. If you do, lucky you!

Let's go on a journey to meet your inner lover. This type of internal adventure is most meaningful when the conscious mind is relaxed, so you can let the subconscious lead in a semi-dreamlike state. To surrender into this experience, you have options: you can have a friend guide you through the journey, you can record it on your phone and play it back, or you can read it through a couple of times and practice from memory.

The "she/her" pronoun and female genitalia are used in this journey. Please change to reflect whatever feels right to you.

 GUIDED VISUALIZATION to Meet Your Inner Lover

- Please use one of the previous practices in this playbook (or one of your own) to relax fully into this moment now. Feel the support of the earth underneath you. Let go further.

- Direct your awareness to drop like an anchor and settle into your belly. Place one hand on your heart and the other on your pussy. Breathe. Soften. Open.

- Notice where you feel a spark, a tingle, a yummy sensation. Often, our inner lovers reside in our hearts or our genitals. But not always.

- Ask your inner lover to reveal herself to you in some way. You may wish to do a P-Pump and get some shakti energy rolling to help draw your inner lover out.

- Once you've located her, and again it may be a tingle or some other subtle knowing, begin to breathe her up. Gently, lovingly encourage her to move toward your head on the inside of your body.

- In your mind's eye, imagine your inner lover being breathed up through your throat. Then, with another breath, she is breathed into your mouth. Maybe she's dancing or lounging on your tongue.

- As your inner lover explores the cavity of your mouth, either literally or in your mind's eye, cup your hands together open to the sky and hold them out in front of you.

- Take another inhale, as you gently exhale through an open mouth, your inner lover floats out of your mouth and lands softly in your hands.

- She is being held with tenderness in a very safe place, your precious hands. Observe her. Notice how you feel as you fully take her in.

- Your inner lover may have been hidden for quite a while. Give her time to adjust to being seen. Be patient. Be curious. Be receptive.

- When she's ready, watch your inner lover leap out of your hands and into a lush meadow full of wildflowers, a sensuous temple of eroticism, or into some other place that brings her pleasure. If your inner lover prefers to stay nestled in your hands, that's just fine.

- Notice how she moves, how she expresses herself, how she plays, what she feels. Take note of as much detail as you can.

- Watch as she blossoms open into being more sensually expressed. What does that look like? How do you feel as you witness her? Allow her to express herself with abandon.

- Ask her what she wants. Invite her to share her fantasies and desires with you. Ask if she has a name.

- Is there anything she'd like to tell you? Listen with an open heart and mind.

- Spend as much time with her as you like. Before you leave, tell her how grateful you are for this connection. Also, be sure to tell her when you'll next check in on her.

- Slowly shift your awareness to your breath. Take as much time as you'd like to follow the breath. When you're ready, begin to let a little light into your eyes and bring yourself back.

Make notes or sketches in the following journal page about your encounter with your inner lover.

Meeting my inner lover

I've already introduced you to my inner lover, Vivacious Viv. My inner lover and wild sensual self are one and the same. Viv is the part of me who most often inspires a Solo Sure. If you have both an inner lover *and* a wild sensual self in your inner pantheon, may I recommend a Solo Sure ménage à trois? OOLALALALALALA!

Now that you've met your inner lover, let's study self-love.

☆ Self-Love Feedback Loop ☆

"All unconditional love begins with love of self. Changing your vibrational awareness, raising your love level, is the only thing that results in any real change. The real motivation to love oneself is that you will not lift your present vibration until you love yourself just the way you are now! Unconditional love is a self-reinforcing system of evolution that begins and ends with loving the self. There is no way around this gateway."

—*Alchemy of Ecstasy* by Ariel Spilsbury

Loving and accepting yourself signals to your psyche that you are worthy and that you are enough just as you are. Wherever you currently are on the self-love and acceptance spectrum, take note because that will change as you practice a Solo Sure. Don't take my word for it. Test it out for yourself.

Where are you, right now, on the spectrum of self-love?

Are you feeling the love and on the "Wildly in Love" end of the range? Are you flooded with self-criticism and on the "Inner Critic on Steroids" end? Or are you somewhere in between?

After you practice a Solo Sure, locate yourself once again on the spectrum of self-love. You can also check throughout the day. If you're not where you want to be, do one of the self-love practices in this chapter or make one up. Remember, if your intention is to fall more deeply in love with you, bring your attention to that intention. With patience and practice, love will abound.

⭐ Let's Get this Sure Thing Going ⭐

I recommend you follow the same steps regardless of whether you're practicing solo or with a partner. That is, get clear on your intention. Then, create an altar. Finally, commit to your weekly practice by marking it in your calendar and deliberately setting aside time. Be sure to let your inner lover know when you've scheduled your Sure Thing because you won't want them to miss it.

If you and your inner lover are ready and don't require anything else (except maybe some lube), skip down to the *Let's Go!* section for some inspiration, or just get to it and enjoy your Solo Sure.

⭐ Getting Intentional ⭐

An intention is a vision, a prayer, an aspiration, a wish. It is the underlying motivation catalyzing your practice. My Sure Thing intention is to deepen in intimacy, connection, and pleasure. Whenever I bring it into my awareness, I think, "Oh yeah, I want that!"

If you're practicing with a partner, you may each have your own intentions, or you may share one. Go with what feels good and right.

Your intention may already be crystal clear. If it is, great. If it's not, try one or more of the options below to gain clarity.

Option A:
If you have a meditation practice or other practice to settle and ground yourself, do it. Afterwards, ask yourself, "What is my intention for a Sure Thing practice?" Listen with your belly and your heart. Allow a response to arise from your body, rather than from your head. Be open to any colors, images, symbols, or words that come. I suggest letting yourself feel into their meaning, rather than getting too analytical.

Option B:
Set some time aside to reveal your intention. In other words, set an intention to receive your Sure Thing intention.

1. Sit comfortably. Bring your awareness to your breath.

2. On the inhale, notice the rise of your belly and then your chest. On the exhale, notice the fall of your chest and then your belly. Repeat.

3. If your mind wanders—and it will!—gently bring it back to the rise and fall of your chest with your breath. Continue this practice until your thoughts become more spacious, your nervous system settles, and you feel relatively centered and grounded.

4. Ask yourself, "What is my intention for a Sure Thing practice?"

5. Listen with your belly and your heart. Allow a response to arise from your body rather than your head. Be open to any colors, images, symbols, or words that come. Let yourself feel into their meaning.

Option C:
While you are in a moment of ecstasy—which may be in the bath, dancing, running, making love, making art, or any other activity that brings you into a state of euphoria—ask yourself, "What is my intention for a Sure Thing practice?" Allow a response to arise from your belly or heart.

Once you have your intention, enter it into the following scroll:

My Sure Thing intention is...

⭐ Altar Creation ⭐

Altars amplify intentions. They are also physical reminders of our dreams and visions that can inspire action, creativity, and pleasure. I recommend creating an altar to support your Solo Sure. It can be as simple or ornate as you'd like. For more on altars and how to create one, check out "Altar Creation" in the *Resources* section.

⭐ Let's Go! ⭐

You've reserved time in your schedule for a Solo Sure, and that time is *now*. Your Solo Sure is about fulfilling *your* intention. Your intention may be to fall more in love with yourself and your body. Or it may be discovering what turns you on. You may want to expand your experience of orgasm. You may wish to access a state of ecstasy in a moment's notice. Like me, your intention may be deepening in pleasure, intimacy, and connection. Whatever your intention is, be aware of it as you enjoy your Sure Thing.

Start by asking yourself or your inner lover or your wild sensual self, "What would be most pleasurable right now?" And follow your own internal pleasure trail to see where it leads you.

⭐ Experiment with Pushing the Limits of Ecstasy ⭐

Sometimes I reach a state of ecstasy that almost feels like too much, on the razor's edge of pleasure and pain. There are two approaches I've found to occupy my mind while continuing to expand my capacity for bodily sensation. I used both of these during labor to manage the pain when I birthed my son at home.

Instead of contracting from ecstatic physical experience or ending it, give your mind something to do. Shift your attention from the deluge of sensation into an exploration of sensation.

⭐ Diving & Dissolving into Sensation ⭐

When you reach a point where it seems you can't possibly take any more sensation,

1. Dive your awareness into the body part experiencing the most intense sensation (i.e., clitoris, G-spot, nipple, glans, anus). Imagine you're a deep-sea diver with a single pointed focus. Continue to dive your attention deeper until it may feel like you have become the sensation.

2. Imagine the boundaries of your physical body dissolving. Place your attention on your entire body as it softens and melts. The edges of your body may disappear. The point of intense sensation gets smaller and fainter. Breathe with the sensation.

In both instances, it feels like I've merged with the sensation in my body, which no longer feels like too much. When I use the first approach, I imagine getting smaller and smaller, as my attention dives deeper. With the second approach, I grow larger and larger as my attention broadens out.

When you feel as if you've plateaued and the sensation is steady or even diminished, begin to pleasure yourself once again. As you reach another peak where you feel you can't take the pleasure one moment longer, again play with diving and dissolving into sensation.

 EXERCISE 11: Ice Cube Play

Let's experiment with diving and dissolving into sensation with an ice cube.

Diving Into Sensation

1. Get an ice cube and hold it in the palm of your hand until it feels uncomfortable.

2. Breathe slowly and deliberately.

3. When it seems impossible to continue to hold the ice cube, bring your attention to the sensation.

4. Keep a single pointed focus as you dive your awareness deeper into the cold.

5. What do you notice? Does the sensation change?

Dissolving Into Sensation

1. Move the ice cube to your other palm.

2. Breathe slowly and deliberately.

3. When it seems impossible to continue to hold the ice cube, bring your attention to your entire body.

4. Imagine the edges of your body diffusing. Feel your body expand as the coldness in your palm becomes a smaller and smaller part of your perception.

5. What do you notice? Does the sensation change?

As you explore how sensation moves and changes in your body, don't be surprised if you unearth other ways to expand your capacity for ecstasy.

⭐ A Solo Sure in Action ⭐

The Solo Sure can be practiced in a multitude of ways. Listed below are some ways to explore the endless universe of pleasure. Allow your creative expression to be roused, your inner lover to be unleashed, and your freak to peak, because this is *all* for *you!*

- ♥ With a feather, tickle stroke your body. Notice which parts are most sensitive. Use your breath to help soften and expand if the sensation feels overwhelming.

- ♥ Give yourself a breast massage with lotion, oil, or my fave, Breast Silk by Garden of Eden Apothecary. Maybe squeeze your nipples. Vary your touch.

- ♥ Drip warm oil on your breasts, belly, and other parts of your body.

- ♥ Massage your body with an oil or lotion you adore. Use intentional touch. Can your hand feel as good as the part of your body it's massaging?

- ♥ Write a love letter to your pussy or cock.

- ♥ Have your pussy or cock write a love letter to you.

- ♥ Give yourself a deliberate orgasm. "DO Date Instructions" are in the *Resources* section.

- ♥ Discover different erogenous zones in your body: nipples, inner thighs, anus, tongue, third eye, etc. With the goal of feeling every stroke, set an alarm for 5, 10, or even 30 minutes. Take yourself on a pleasure ride. Bring yourself up and down as you explore which areas of your body bring you the most pleasure.

- ♥ In a bath or shower, experiment with the water as it gushes out of the faucet or shower head and saturates different parts of your body.

- ♥ Do any part or the entirety of the *Pleasure Fit for a Goddess* experience in Chapter 9.

- ♥ Choose one sense that you'll be immersing yourself in. You may want to plan for 5 weeks in a row, where each week during your Solo Sure you explore taste, touch, smell, sound, or sight. Or you could do a combination of any of them.

- ♥ Get out a hand mirror and admire the delicate folds of your labia or shape of your scrotum.

- ♥ In a full-length mirror, seduce yourself. Striptease, if you please.

☆ Judgment Alert ☆

If you start to hear a barrage of mean comments from a voice in your head (i.e., "Look at that fat ______", "I hate my ______," "You'll never get this."). That's a signal to STOP. RIGHT. THERE.

Intrinsic to a Solo Sure practice is the cultivation of self-love. That includes learning to accept those parts of you that can be mean and self-critical. I know it sounds counterintuitive to turn towards the parts that feel icky. After all, this is supposed to be about pleasure.

The truth is, the more you get to know and ultimately accept the parts of yourself that you judge and consider ugly or unwanted, the less these aspects act out. As you love yourself into wholeness, the critical voices in your head get softer and surface less often. As you get to know these parts more, you'll notice when they arrive on the scene. When they do, turn toward them and invite them for a cup of tea or even a hug. And of course, when you realize they have the mic, lovingly take the mic and give it to someone else in your inner pantheon.

The point is, the more familiar you are with your inner world, the more agile you will be to switch your mind on a dime. Now that's empowering!

As per usual, you have choices. You may wish to take yourself on a guided journey from judging to loving. Or you may feel drawn to the open-eyed meditation option. Or you may wish to go on a playdate with your inner critic. Or any combination of the three.

♡ Guided Visualization ♡

This type of internal adventure is most meaningful when the conscious mind is relaxed, so you can let the subconscious lead in a semi-dreamlike state. To surrender into this experience, you have options: you can have a friend guide you through the journey, you can record it on your phone and play it back, or you can read it through a couple of times and practice from memory.

Also, this is a journey you may wish to take more than once, and even many times.

☆ Journey from Judging to Loving ☆

- Make sure you are in a comfortable position. You may want to lie down.
- Please use one of the previous practices in this playbook (or one of your own) to relax fully into this moment now. Feel the support of the earth underneath you. Then, let go further.
- Allow your awareness to become like an anchor. Feel, see, sense your attention move down your body into your belly and genitals.
- Take a few deep breaths and see the anchor of your awareness drop deeper into the unknown. Relax and let go.
- Allow one thing you admire about yourself to bubble up in your mind. One thing that's easy for you to like. It could be a character in your inner pantheon.
- Now, invite in one or two other aspects of yourself that you appreciate, even love about yourself. Again, these could be characters in your inner pantheon.
- Increase the feelings of acceptance and appreciation you feel for these parts of you. Let this feeling grow and seep into your entire body.
- As you bask in unconditional acceptance, allow a part of you to come to mind that you've judged in the past, but have come to accept. Perhaps you judged a character in your inner pantheon, a physical trait, a habit you had, or some way that you are.
- Where did the criticism come from? Was it a societal ideal? Someone else's judgment of you that you adopted? Or something else?

- In your mind's eye, let unfold the journey from judging this part of self to accepting this part of self. How did it happen? Invite memories to flood in that you may perceive details that contributed to you accepting this part of yourself.
- Return in your mind's eye to the one, two, or three parts of yourself you appreciate that you already identified. Maybe they are dancing or spiraling around you. Maybe they are holding you, hugging you, or some other way of loving you up.
- While basking in this nourishing party of acceptance, bring to mind something about yourself you currently judge. Again, it could be a character in your inner pantheon, a physical trait, a habit you have, or some way that you are. Anything that you currently judge about yourself.
- Where does the criticism come from? Is it a societal ideal? Someone else's judgment of you that you adopted? Or something else?
- As you rest your attention on this part that you judge, notice if you see anything differently. Maybe something is illuminated you hadn't seen before.
- Bring back into focus a part of you that you love and accept. And, if that feels at all challenging, instead, bring to mind someone who is easy for you to love. Just the thought of them melts open your heart and brings a smile.
- Slowly shift your awareness to your breath. Take as much time as you'd like to follow the breath. When you're ready, begin to let a little light into your eyes and bring yourself back.

Make notes or sketches in the following journal page about what you discovered.

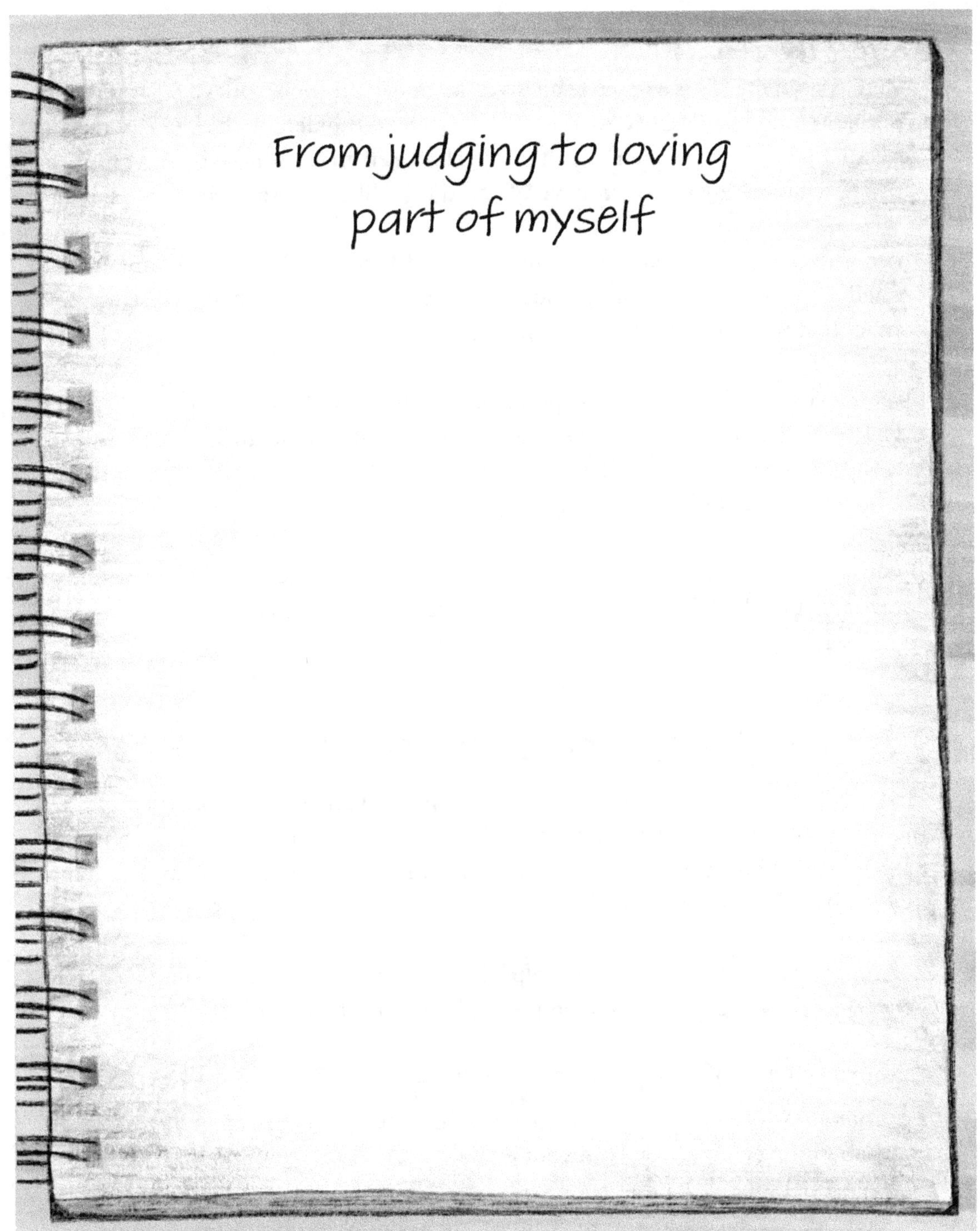
From judging to loving
part of myself

⭐ Personal Share ⭐

When I was in my 20s, I worked at an investment bank in New York City. I remember wishing I could be like my co-workers who seemed fulfilled by the work of closing deals that made rich people richer. I judged how sensitive I was. Why can't I just be satisfied with making lots of money? Why did I feel like something in me was dying?

To endure that job for four years, Disconnected D most often had the mic. D was created when I was very young and didn't want to feel the judgment, stress, and conflict that was prevalent in my nuclear family.

Over the years as I've engaged the practices in this book, I have grown to accept and even love D. When I notice I've disassociated, I now have strategies to bring me back into my body. I may bring my hands to my heart and belly, bring my attention to the bottom of my feet, or lightly slap my thighs.

Because of loving D into wholeness, I'm able to glean the gifts of my sensitive, somatic nature. And that has certainly enhanced my ability to make choices that are right for me.

💜 EXERCISE 12: Mirroring Self-Acceptance 💜

First, read through the entire exercise a few times. Then enact it from memory. Do the best you can to recall the specifics of the exercise, but don't focus on getting it exactly right. Allow yourself to surrender to your own inner knowing and guidance as you mirror self-acceptance.

As you do this exercise, it may be helpful to imagine yourself becoming a channel between earth and sky, open and empty, with no expectations.

1. Sit or stand comfortably in front of a mirror.

2. Look into your eyes. Breathe with yourself. Soften your gaze and relax while still maintaining connection with your eyes.

3. Allow thoughts to float by like a cloud. If you notice your mind grasping onto a thought or storyline, stay with your eyes, as you inhale, think, "EMPTY." As you exhale, think, "EMPTY."

4. Imagine a giant magnet in the center of the earth. This magnet draws thoughts and emotions from your mind and body. Inhale and exhale "EMPTY."

5. Repeat Steps 3 and 4 as you notice stray thoughts or emotions arise.

6. Maintain your gaze and breathe into your heart. Continue until you feel an opening and/or softening in your heart. Enjoy this connection with yourself.

7. If you'd like, bow to yourself. Then, rest your gaze on some part of your body that you are currently able to appreciate. It may be the curve of your chin, the curl of your hair, the shape of your forearm, the length of your fingers, the dimple on your cheek.

8. Then, wherever your gaze lands on your body, find something you can honestly admire and be grateful for. Speak your appreciation out loud if that feels good. For instance: "I like the way my hip curves out into my ass." "I find comfort in the swell of my belly." "I like the color of my eyes." "I appreciate my legs for taking me where I want to go."

9. Then, move your gaze to another part of your body that you are able to accept exactly as it is. Repeat as many times as you'd like.

10. If critical thoughts or emotions arise, return to steps 3 and 4 and EMPTY.

⭒ Playdate with Your Inner Critic ⭒

We all have aging bodies. One of the secrets to aging gracefully is to accept your changing body. This is a tall order in the puritanical patriarchy we live in, as we unpacked in Chapter 3. However, as we courageously turn toward our own and society's judgments about our bodies with compassion and acceptance, we create a new paradigm of self-love. As we act from a place of unconditional self-love, it ripples out into our relationships, our communities, and the world.

Of course, this new paradigm begins with self-acceptance. I've discovered play to be a potent path to accepting what is.

If I find myself judging the loose skin that now hangs off my neck, I bring myself out of my mind and into my body. First, I may touch the skin. How does it feel? Soft. Warm. Maybe I change the pressure of my touch or tickle the skin. Then, I may turn my head from side to side to see how my neck skin changes. Perhaps I get a hand mirror so I can get a different view of it. Or maybe I swallow or eat a bite of food and watch how the loose skin reacts.

If judgmental thoughts arise, I notice them. Then, I turn my attention back to the playdate with my neck skin. I'm in a love laboratory experimenting with different means of surrendering to what is.

"How can I accept this?" I wonder.

Just like I accept anything that isn't exactly how I want it to be—initially, I feel resistance and then I soften. The next step is to turn toward whatever it is I resist. In this case, the skin on my neck. So I play with it. Touch it. And, finally, welcome it. Can I truly open my heart to this changing neck and love it just as it is? Sometimes the answer is yes, and sometimes no. No matter. So long as I continue to play and engage, the game is on.

Now it's your turn. If there's a part of your body that you regularly judge, invite in the Muse to inspire a game you can play with this body part. Make it jiggle. Look at it in a mirror while standing on your head. Draw hearts on it with non-toxic paint. Dare to be silly!

☆ Kindness is Key ☆

A Solo Sure practice will connect you with the parts you love and the parts you judge and is a pathway to love yourself into wholeness. Since change is the only reality, and that certainly includes the physical body, the sooner a practice of body acceptance is adopted, the more kind, loving, and pleasurable the experience of aging will be.

Have you checked back in with your inner lover? If not, now's as good a time as any. When I do a P-Pump (Exercise #7 in Chapter 4), Vivacious Viv immediately saunters forward in my consciousness. Try a P-Pump and see if that does it for you. Experiment with what connects *you* with your inner lover.

Most importantly, be kind and patient with yourself as you explore new arenas of pleasure and cultivate your capacity for ecstasy.

Give It Away

"The miracle is this—the more we share, the more we have."
—Leonard Nimoy

💜 Challenge

Share one joyful, love-centered moment from your week (not necessarily sexual) with a friend or family member to normalize pleasure as a force for good.

💜 Challenge Afterglow

How was that for you? What was the other person's response? Was it a conversation opener? Would you do it again?

Love Ripple Challenge Notes

Chapter 8
Ingredients to Sustain Your Practice

If a particular practice feeds your body and soul, make it a priority.
It's that simple.

This chapter provides the basic building blocks for establishing a consistent weekly Sure Thing practice.

Popular culture—through romantic comedies, romance novels, and fairy tales—portrays romantic relationships, pleasure, and sensuality as arising organically. In these depictions, our appetite for sex is a lusty upwelling that magically appears at the perfect moment. Yet anyone who has been in a long-term relationship knows that maintaining ongoing physical intimacy and connection takes dedication.

The Sure Thing is like any growth-engendering practice, be it spiritual, physical, or mental. Your pleasure aspiration will require commitment, effort, and devotion.

But this risks making it sound a lot less fun than it actually is. After all, your commitment and effort are in service to pleasure and intimacy! So don't be discouraged. There's a tantalizing payoff for the "work"—and in my experience, once there's a certain momentum, considerably less effort is required. The "discipline" required rapidly becomes natural—because this is a practice *you will want to do!*

And like any practice, it rests on a foundation: commitment.

✧ Commitment ✧

The word alone can bring stuff up. Notice what happens as you read it—what thoughts, images, feelings, or sensations arise when you encounter the word *commitment*? Jot them down on the following journal page.

There are three ingredients I consider essential to any commitment: trust, surrender, and courage. When you commit to something, you both release and receive: you let go of one possibility while gaining another. For instance, if you commit to a Sure Thing practice, the time you devote to it replaces something else you might have done—but in exchange, you're investing in fulfilling your intention.

There's a tricky bit to this. You may not know all you'll need to give up when you make a commitment. And, while you likely have a sense of what you stand to gain, you can never know for sure. If you did know, there would be no need to practice trust and surrender into the unknown—which takes courage.

Bring to mind a commitment you've made that has been fulfilling. Write about it in the following journal page.

When I hear the word
"commitment" I think of...

A commitment that was
fulfilling to me was...

When Bill and I became serious, I felt no pull toward marriage. I'd already been married once and felt no need to do it again. But when we began our journey to parenthood, Bill wanted to get engaged. When he proposed, I accepted, knowing I wanted to spend my life with him.

A couple of years passed, and I still wasn't pregnant. Even so, it felt right to honor our bond with a formal ceremony. The morning after our wedding day, I woke up feeling different. What changed? I wondered. And then I realized: a back door in my psyche—one I hadn't even realized was standing open—had slammed shut.

I knew I was giving up sex with others when I married Bill. But I did not realize I was also closing the back door protecting my heart. My secret escape route was so well-hidden I myself hadn't realized it existed. This psychic hedge was only apparent *after* I made the commitment. But at the same time, I soon realized, I'd gained the thrill of fully opening my heart to him.

And that's not all I gained.

As fate would have it, the first time I ovulated after we got married, our son was conceived!

⭐ Your Turn ⭐

Reflect on a fulfilling commitment you've made. What challenges did you overcome to be able to commit? How did you overcome them? What did you let go of that you might not have known you were holding onto? Were there surprising outcomes? How has that commitment enhanced your life?

Capture your responses in the following journal page.

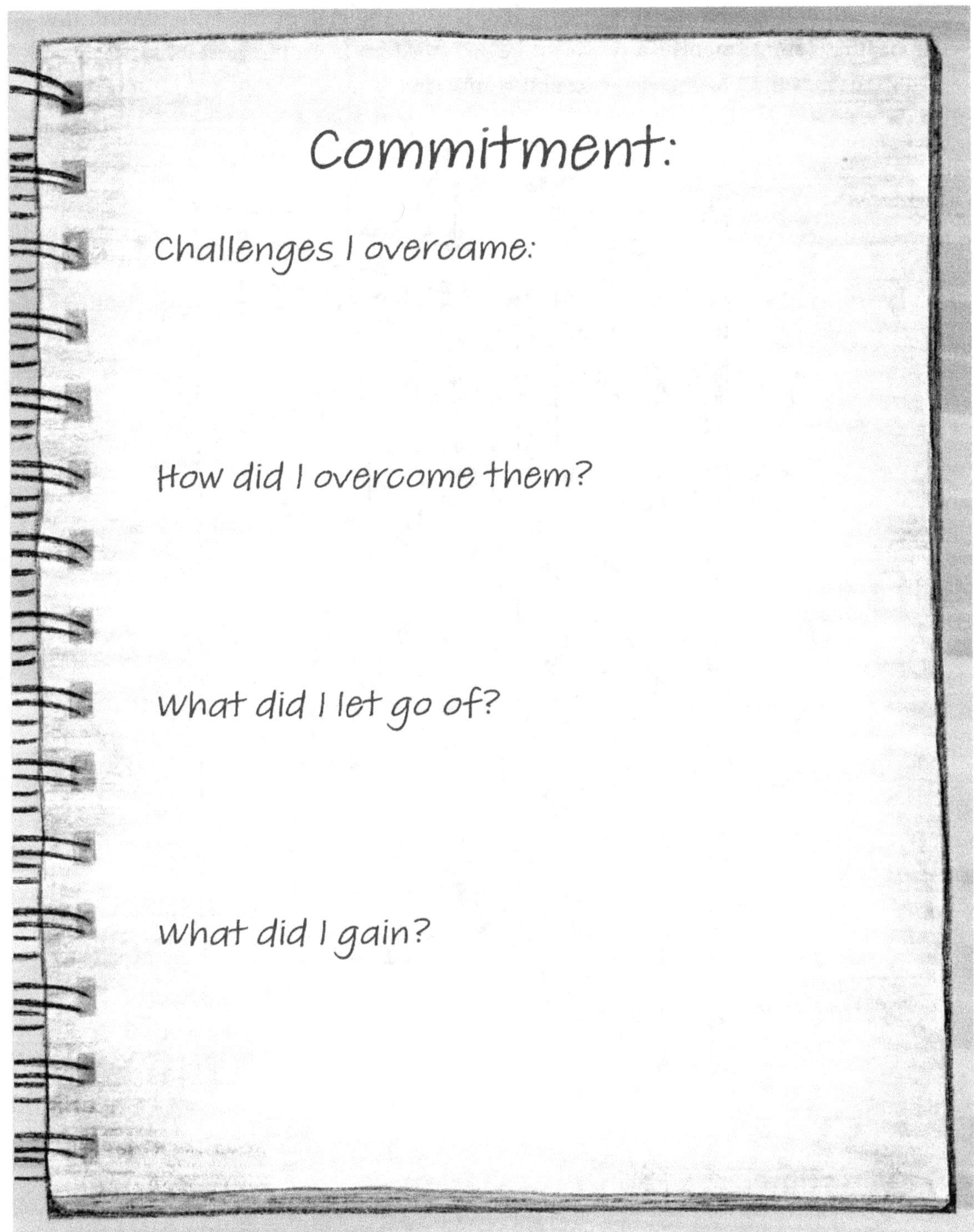
Commitment:

Challenges I overcame:

How did I overcome them?

what did I let go of?

what did I gain?

Commitment is often perceived as a ball and chain. But in reality, it is quite the opposite. Commitment is a powerful key to freedom from the prisons in our lives constructed out of fear, resistance, and complacency.

Commitment is the soil in which the seeds of intimacy, sensuality, and pleasure can grow. It requires stepping into the unknown, which itself calls for trust, surrender, and courage.

 Effort

In addition to commitment, effort is needed for a successful ongoing practice. Effort can be pleasurable, like the rush of adrenaline during a workout. But effort can also be difficult, like facing a looming deadline when procrastination has crept in.

I myself have a love/hate relationship with effort. At the age of 15, I discovered that exercise lifts my mood. When I'm feeling down and want to raise my spirits, I engage in physical activity. Sometimes it takes effort to get off the couch and stretch or go for a hike. And even once I've started it sometimes feels effortful to continue.

I frequently hike with my dog up a steep fire road. During the uphill climb, I routinely notice the thought, "I don't want to do this." Or "I should just turn back." When I notice the thought, I pause. I take a deep inhale and let it out as I take a step forward. Gently, I remind myself to focus on just the next step, and then the next.

Over time, I've become accustomed to these thoughts. Sometimes I'm able to greet them with a chuckle of recognition. Other times, they feel heavier, so I pause to give myself a moment. I breathe with the resistance and focus on the sensations in my body instead of the thoughts in my head. Inevitably, a short time later, I feel the energy shift, and I resume the effort.

Oftentimes, once I'm in the activity or practice, it kind of generates its own momentum. The most effort is needed to kick it off. That's true with my Sure Thing practice. I'm not always in the mood when the scheduled time to practice has arrived. That's when a little effort is required. I remind myself that all I need to do is answer the question, "What would be most pleasurable right now?"

Presto. A Sure Thing has begun, and the effort falls away.

Your Turn

What is something you do regularly that requires effort? Envision yourself engaged in that activity. What thoughts, specifically, arise to derail you? How do you respond to them? What keeps you going?

Use the following journal page to answer the questions and free write or draw about your experience.

What I'm noticing about effort:

Getting to know your own roadblocks and habits when effort is required will serve you well. As you begin a Sure Thing practice, don't be surprised if the internal voice that tries to sabotage your efforts grows louder and more obvious.

Once you notice undermining thoughts and recognize them for what they are, you have options:

1. Firmly and intentionally turn your attention toward what it is you want, and away from the disempowering thoughts.

2. Name that voice in your head and add another character to your inner pantheon. Then, consciously take the mic away and give it to a different character in your inner pantheon, perhaps your inner lover or wild sensual self.

Another factor that has dramatically reduced the effort required for my weekly Sure Thing is understanding the difference between spontaneous and responsive desire.

⭐ Spontaneous vs. Responsive Desire ⭐

I'd always thought sexual intimacy began with an eruption of desire in me or my partner. Turns out I fell for the Hollywood narrative, in which all sex occurs spontaneously.

Spontaneous desire is characterized by a sudden, unprompted urge for sexual activity. Perhaps you see someone you find sexy and think, "I'm really hot for you. Let's get naked!" Or out of nowhere you have a sexual thought and want sex. That's *spontaneous* desire.

Then there's responsive desire, where arousal and desire are dependent on context, affection, sensual touch, or other physical stimuli. Responsive desire is born out of pleasure. For example, a special someone begins to massage your shoulders. As you relax, they lean in and nuzzle your neck with their nose. Your body responds and you think, "This feels good. I like this person. Let's make out." That's *responsive* desire. "Where spontaneous desire appears in *anticipation* of pleasure, responsive desire emerges in *response* to pleasure."[16]

The same person can experience spontaneous desire at some points and responsive desire at others—and this can shift with different partners or under different circumstances.

Until a few years ago, I primarily felt spontaneous desire. Before I knew about responsive desire, when it was time for our Sure Thing and I wasn't turned on, I would feel heaviness and resistance. Learning about responsive desire was a game-changer. The resistance disappeared, along with the need to be aroused.

Desire can be the spark for your Sure Thing. But if it's not present, don't worry—pleasure can lead you there.

 Devotion

Along with commitment and effort, devotion is a necessary ingredient for any regular practice. I initially called this section "discipline," and then a friend suggested I instead use the word "devotion." Which prompted me to look up *discipline*. I learned that it is defined as the practice of training people to obey rules or a code of behavior, using punishment to correct disobedience. Yikes!

My friend was absolutely right. Discipline definitely shouldn't be part of a Sure Thing practice. Devotion, on the other hand, is defined as love, loyalty, or enthusiasm for a person, activity, or cause. Now that's more like it.

Like every practice I've ever engaged in—and there have been many—devotion is a primary factor. I think of devotion as the scaffolding for practice. Before a building is constructed, scaffolding must be erected to provide the workers with safety, access, and support to do their work.

My longest-running daily practice is seated meditation. For over 20 years, the scaffolding that has supported this practice is an altar and sitting cushions in my bedroom. This serves as a reminder to get my butt on that cushion each day.

Your Turn

Choose one activity or practice in your life that requires ongoing devotion. What helps you to continue to engage in it? Do you have an accountability pal? A coach? Physical objects that support you? How do you nurture your devotion?

Use the following journal page to write or draw about how devotion shows up in your life.

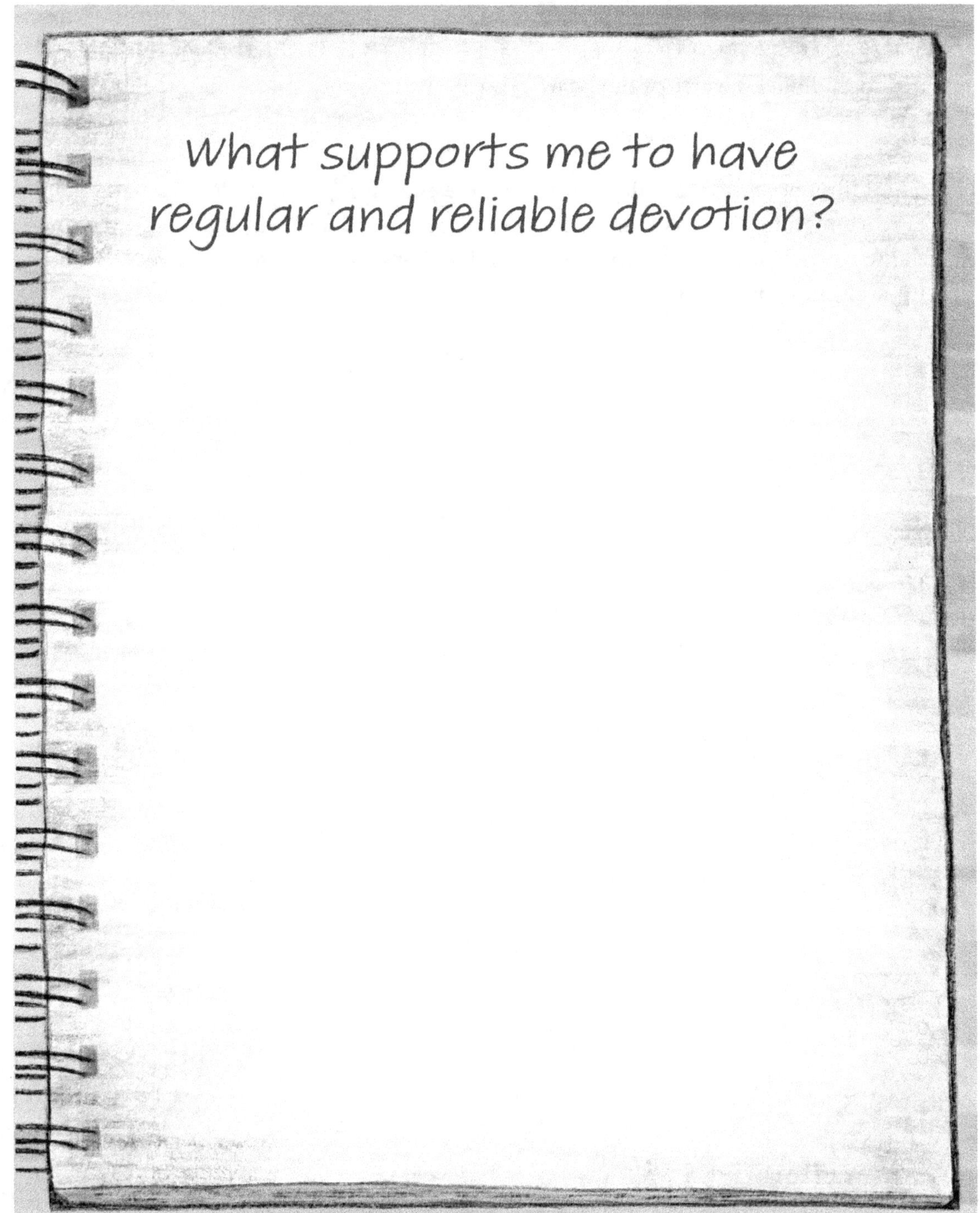
What supports me to have
regular and reliable devotion?

Devotion is an expression of love. It is an honoring of something that inspires you and makes your heart sing. As Rumi said, "With every breath, I plant the seeds of devotion; I am a farmer of the heart." Devotion is serving something you love with love.

Commitment, effort, and devotion are the essential ingredients for realizing your Sure Thing intention. As you practice, you'll learn to dance with them, discovering the unique rhythms—the twirls, dips, and sashays—that make your practice both fulfilling and consistent.

Responsive Desire on Blast

"Pleasure is the measure. Wanting sex is not the central feature of sexual well-being, liking the sex you have is."
—Emily Nagoski

The pharmaceutical industry treats women who don't experience spontaneous desire as a medical problem, marketing "female viagra" as the solution. Now you know better. Please share the good news about responsive desire.

♡ Challenge

Educate your friends about the science of desire: spontaneous vs. responsive desire. Spontaneous desire is when you suddenly desire sex. Responsive desire is when desire arises from pleasure or from context. Both are normal and healthy, and neither is better than the other. You may experience either one or both, depending on the circumstances.

♡ Challenge Afterglow

How did your friends respond? Did they know about responsive desire? How was it for you to share about this?

Love Ripple Challenge Notes

Chapter 9
Primed, Prepped, and Ready

The more we practice kindness, the more often we'll respond with love.

This chapter sets the stage for your Sure Thing practice, offering guidance for the immediate lead-up to a Sure Thing. Here you'll find personal, partner, and ritual preparations, along with potential obstacles to overcome and thresholds to cross. It also includes a range of methods to warm up with yourself and/or your partner. Lastly, you may want to check out the "Essentials" section of the *Resources* chapter as part of your preparations.

As always, if something doesn't feel right, skip it. And, of course, include your own ideas. Remember: the only limitation is imagination, which means there are no limits.

And if you're already randy, then go ahead and get on with your Sure Thing! And you can save this chapter for another day.

⭐ Ritual Pleasure Prep ⭐

I recommend you follow the same steps regardless of whether you're practicing solo or with a partner. First, get clear on your intention. Next, create an altar. Finally, commit to your weekly practice by setting aside a regular time and marking it in your calendar.

So it all begins with setting a clear and simple intention. If you've already done this in Chapter 7, I suggest checking back in with that intention to be sure it still resonates.

⭐ Getting Intentional ⭐

An intention is a vision, a prayer, an aspiration, a wish. It is the underlying motivation catalyzing your practice. My Sure Thing intention is to deepen in intimacy, connection, and pleasure. Whenever I bring it into my awareness, I think, "Oh yeah, I want that!"

If you're practicing with a partner, you may each have your own intentions, or you may share one. Go with what feels good and right.

Your intention may already be crystal clear. If it is, great. If it's not, try one or more of the options below to gain clarity.

Option A:
If you have a meditation practice or other practice to settle and ground yourself, do it. Afterwards, ask yourself, "What is my intention for a Sure Thing practice?" Listen with your belly and your heart. Allow a response to arise from your body, rather than from your head. Be open to any colors, images, symbols, or words that come. I suggest letting yourself feel into their meaning, rather than getting too analytical.

Option B:
Set some time aside to reveal your intention. In other words, set an intention to receive your Sure Thing intention.

1. Sit comfortably. Bring your awareness to your breath.

2. On the inhale, notice the rise of your belly and then your chest. On the exhale, notice the fall of your chest and then your belly. Repeat.

3. If your mind wanders—and it will!—gently bring it back to the rise and fall of your chest with your breath. Continue this practice until your thoughts become more spacious, your nervous system settles, and you feel relatively centered and grounded.

4. Ask yourself, "What is my intention for a Sure Thing practice?"

5. Listen with your belly and your heart. Allow a response to arise from your body rather than your head. Be open to any colors, images, symbols, or words that come. Let yourself feel into their meaning.

Option C:
While you are in a moment of ecstasy—which may be in the bath, dancing, running, making love, making art, or any other activity that brings you into a state of

euphoria—ask yourself, "What is my intention for a Sure Thing practice?" Allow a response to arise from your belly or heart.

Once you have your intention, enter it into the scroll below.

If this section rings a bell, good—you're paying attention! A clear and strong intention is such a vital foundation for practice that I've included the same series of inquiries here and in Chapter 7.

✬ Visual Representation of Your Intention ✬

On my bedroom wall is a drawing of a man lying on a field of wildflowers, a woman lying on top of him, and flowers sprouting between them. Every time I see it, I feel a tingle of turn-on.

Having an image that elicits *your* Sure Thing intention will support your practice. It can be something you create yourself, such as a collage, a drawing, a painting, a photograph, or even a tapestry. Maybe you already have an image that reflects your intention perfectly. Or you might look through files, magazines, or digital archives to find one. Or you may wish to ask an artist to create an image for you, as I did.

The piece of visual art could be the centerpiece of your Sure Thing altar, or it could be the altar itself. The purpose of the altar is to inspire you to practice while keeping your Sure Thing commitment present in your life. An altar will both amplify and magnetize your intention. Check out "Altar Creation" in the *Resources* section of this playbook for more tips and direction.

⭐ Solo Practices: What Gets You in the Mood? ⭐

When the partner of a friend of mine was eager to make love, he would draw her a bath when she came home from work. He knew that my friend would be more open to his advances if she first had a leisurely soak in the tub. Another friend trained her spouse to anoint her body with essential oils as the entrée into foreplay. For her, if there were no oils, she was a "no thank you."

What encourages the delicate petals of *your* sensual self to open? What helps you release and surrender into pleasure? What do you need to truly relax and let go?

Most of us will require a deliberate transition from the mundane tasks of our everyday lives into the sanctum of the sensual world. What helps you change the channel? After a long day of work or caretaking, what will pleasurably shift you from a more head-centered space to a body-centered space? What is it *you* require to open your sensory self to explore intimacy and pleasure?

If you don't know, experiment! Try a massage, a bath, a scrumptious bite to eat, a scent that intoxicates you. Or a sensuous dance, stimulating music, a foot rub— anything that seems pleasing.

Make notes and/or drawings in the following journal page about things that open you sensually.

Some ways that help me
soften in my body are...

Honestly, sometimes I just don't feel like it. I'd rather just go to sleep or veg out with a show or a book. Who needs this Sure Thing anyway? But then something inside me—sometimes it's just a faint whisper—says "I do!" I know that if I keep my commitment to this practice, it will enrich me, my relationship, and my life. When I meditate, practice yoga, or train in aikido, I never get up off the cushion or mat and think, "That was a waste of time." The same has been true for my Sure Thing practice.

☆ Please~O~Meter: Activate to Titillate! ☆

Whether you have a Solo Sure practice or you simply want to fluff up your turn-on before your partner joins in, below is a menu of pleasure-inducing choices to get the ecstasy rolling. Partake in as many as you'd like. The only key is to follow your desire and your please~o~meter—yep, that's your inner pleasure meter.

My wish for you is that these practices deepen your connection, acceptance, and love for the body that you inhabit. It's the only one you've got—so why not treat it as the amazing creation it is?

⋆ P-Pump ⋆

First, there's the Pelvic Pump, from Chapter 4. Since it's such a simple and profound practice, I'll describe it briefly again. The Pelvic Pump (P-Pump) is an easy way to awaken the ecstatic energy at the base of the spine. Lift your pelvic floor and hold for 3-5 seconds. You may also want to squeeze the anus as well as the labia, should you have a pussy. Experiment with different holds, different lengths of time, and different numbers of pumps. One pump may be all you want, or thirteen pumps may be your lucky number. Notice the energy as it moves through your body. Follow your body's delight.

⋆ Making Love in Your Mouth ⋆

Another delectable practice is the tongue lovemaking technique. Begin by gently licking the inside of your mouth with the tip of your tongue. Lick around the teeth, the upper palate, the gums. Play with the pressure of the tongue. Go with what feels most pleasurable. Experiment with flicks and longer or shorter strokes. If you dare, peek your tongue out of your mouth and sensuously lick your lips. As you're making love to the cavity of your mouth with your tongue, connect with your genitals. Perhaps do a P-Pump.

As you continue to pleasure your mouth with your tongue, swallow. Follow the energy. Perhaps to your genitals. Notice the effect on the rest of your body as you make love to your mouth with your tongue. Get creative.

⋆ Jade/Crystal Egg-sploration ⋆

This practice is for those with pussies. The heaviness of the egg helps make the pelvic floor stronger and more toned by providing resistance. Benefits of using a crystal egg for up to 10 minutes at a time include increased natural lubrication and increased sensitivity during intercourse. However, if you are someone who has difficulty relaxing your pelvic floor muscles, then the egg may not be appropriate for you.

There are lots of ways to play with a crystal egg. When I'm in the tub, I enjoy placing an egg in my introitus—the largest opening in the pussy. First, I put the egg in my mouth to warm it up. While in my mouth, I infuse the egg with an intention. Then, with that intention in mind, I gently insert the egg. While in the tub, I may lift and lower the egg for various lengths of time, or I may just relax and enjoy the sensation of the egg inside of me.

To remove the egg: sometimes it pops out when I get out of the tub. If not, I find it easiest to squat down and push.

⭐ Tune In Creatively to Turn On ⭐

Do a sensual dance, draw the nude body, write erotic poetry, or engage in any form of creativity that gets your juices pumping. What is a joyful form of expression for you? If you don't yet know, let this be an invitation to discover something wonderful about yourself!

Then, there's taking in erotica created by someone else: poetry, short stories, art, graphic novels, and soft porn. Experiment. Keep an open mind. If something feels taboo, pay attention. Who in your inner pantheon thinks it's taboo? Perhaps your inner lover or wild sensual self would like to take the mic.

Finally, there's an extravagant practice I adapted from Erwan Davon's "Visiting Dignitary." Be forewarned, this practice will encourage you to love your body just as it is. According to Emily Nagoski, "Women will not be fully, blissfully satisfied with their sex lives until they are fully, blissfully satisfied with their own bodies."[17]

WARNING: If at any point in your research your inner critic won't give up the mic, STOP. RIGHT. THERE. I suggest you go immediately to the *Judgment Alert* section in Chapter 7.

☆ Pleasure Fit for a God/dess ☆

Allow at least one hour, and that may be rushing it. If you have a partner who shares the same space, ask for privacy while you indulge yourself. There is no right order in which to do this practice, so I encourage you to look at the instructions, and then find your own way with it. Also, change the pronouns to suit you.

Visit from your Inner Lover

This exploration is all about you. You get to create a luxuriously sensual space specifically for your inner lover. Imagine you are seducing her into full embodiment and expression. How does she want to be seduced? What flowers, smells, tastes, sounds, textures, and colors does she prefer? You may wish to include all of the senses while creating your den of sumptuous sensuality.

Dim the lights, put on sexy music, toss colorful pillows on your bed, adjust the heat, fix your inner lover's favorite food: chocolate, strawberries, seaweed salad… whatever is most likely to tantalize their taste buds. Arrange fresh flowers, light incense, anoint yourself with your favorite essential oil, bring in your favorite faux fur to lie on. In short: do whatever delights and enchants you, because you, my dear, are worth everything it takes to create a luscious temple for your inner lover.

Once you're set up, slowly and intentionally indulge each of your senses. Perhaps try two at a time—like biting into something delicious while caressing your breast. Or let your body dissolve into a song as you inhale the scent of a flower or herb. Try out some creative combinations of your own.

Visual Seduction

Now that your senses have been aroused, experiment with seductive glances, looks, and postures. You'll need a full-length mirror and a hand mirror for this part of the exercise.

First, come into empty presence with yourself in the mirror. Bask in the connection with your essence/soul/authentic self.

What is Empty Presence?
Empty Presence is the foundational practice taught in the 13 Moon Mystery School. The objective is to become a clear channel through which the divine/wisdom/universal truth can move. As we empty ourselves of thoughts, emotions, and movement, this becomes possible.

Imagine yourself to be a reed of consciousness, open and empty, with no expectations. This practice is often done with a partner, using each other's eyes as a portal. For this exercise, you'll be your own partner, working with a mirror about 3 feet away.

Sit comfortably and look into your own eyes. Allow your gaze to soften. Breathe deeply and slowly. Purposefully cross your eyes. This will assist you in letting go of the grip the mind normally keeps on your perception. Continue to breathe deeply. You may begin to see a band of light on one side of your head or the other. Don't force it. It will simply arise in non-focus as you continue to practice. This practice invites you to sustain a laser focus even as, paradoxically, you practice openness and surrender.

Your face may begin to shapeshift. Do your best not to indulge your thinking about any of it. You are training your mind to focus, instead of being absorbed in thoughts. This takes practice. When you notice thoughts arising, use your breath to return to open awareness. You may experience a new state of openness and receptivity, where images, guidance, and symbols arise unbidden.

If you touch into this, you have entered an expanded and coherent field of awareness and resonance. Spend as much time here as you'd like.

Now, remove your clothes as sensuously as you wish while staying present in your body. Take some risks as you undress for your inner lover. Perhaps you add music, then give yourself your most erotic "come hither" look, be a bit of a tease… whatever feels evocative, sexy, and fun.

Once you're undressed, it's time to go into full-on seduction mode. Strike poses, swing your hips, giggle, dance, tease, stretch—whatever helps you more fully embody your seductress self. Turn yourself on, and then see if you can turn it up just a little more!

Touching for the Pleasure of It

Touch various parts of your body. Check in with your inner lover and see where she most wants to be touched, and touch her there. Adjust the pressure. Try something new, touch yourself in a way you've never been touched. Use your fingers, toes, feathers. Let loose your imagination.

Exploring Orgasm

Set yourself up comfortably. Have your favorite lube and sex toys nearby. Be sure that the room's temperature is perfect for you, and that you have plenty of pillows, blankets, and whatever else you need to feel like the recumbent goddess you are. Keep the mirrors close. The goal of this exercise is to open as much as you possibly can to the sensation you create in your body. That means taking your time, enjoying each moment, and expanding the pleasure by trying to feel each and every stroke.

Now, slowly and with your full attention, apply some lube to your genitals. The clitoris is often the most pleasure-inducing part of the pussy, while the head is often the most pleasure-inducing part of the cock. Is this the case for you? Where, specifically, is it most sensitive?

As you stroke yourself, use shorter, quicker strokes to heighten the sensation. Then slow or pause the strokes until the sensation subsides a bit and you feel yourself at a plateau. Then continue. Discover how you most want to be touched.

Perhaps get a sex toy, lube it up, and insert it into your anus or introitus. Push the limits of ecstasy by diving and dissolving into sensation as described in Chapter 7.

Play with *not* taking yourself over the edge. Stop one stroke short if you can and take a bite of a yummy meal you prepared. Does it taste different in this heightened state?

Grab a mirror and check out your genitals. If shame arises, let it know: Not now. You can always go back to the Shedding Shame Shackles exercise in Chapter 3 on page 44. But for now, you're leaning into all the pleasure that you innately deserve.

Back to your gorgeous genitals: What changes do you notice? Gaze into your eyes. What do you see? Connect with your inner lover. Continue for as long as you'd like. There's no limit to the pleasure you can feel if you're willing to soften, open, and surrender.

When you're ready to, bring yourself down with slow, heavy strokes and firm pressure. I like to squeeze my labia together. Discover how *you* like to come down. Make the coming down as deliberate and pleasurable as the going up. Stay awake and connected to the sensations in your body.

Radiant Reception

Standing or lying down, receive yourself in the mirror. Appreciate yourself and your body. Thank it for granting you pleasure. Shower yourself with compliments. *You're smokin' hot. You're a dream come true, babe. Thanks for the ecstasy.*

⭐ Thresholds to Cross & Obstacles to Overcome ⭐

Laziness is an obstacle I encounter with my Sure Thing practice. When I really don't feel like it, I know I need to put in a little effort. So I clear my mind using the breath, movement, or a P-Pump. Then, I focus on my Sure Thing intention. That's all I generally need to do to traverse the laziness threshold. When you feel lazy, what supports you to follow through with your commitments and desires?

Boredom is another threshold I sometimes need to cross to fulfill my Sure Thing commitment. The antidote is mindfulness. "Be here now," Ram Dass famously wrote, and this seemingly simple guidance is a reliable cure for boredom.

There is *literally* nothing like the present moment. Each moment with its innumerable arisings can never be replicated. If you are open to the moment-to-moment, ever-changing nature of reality, I believe it's impossible to be bored.

Here are some ways to play with boredom:

- Notice a few of the multitude of sensory inputs that flood your body every second: through your eyes, your ears, your fingers, your nostrils.
- Watch the endless stream of thoughts that appear out of nowhere.
- Track the shifting energy in the body—where is there tingling, or heat, or pulsing.
- Meditate: Observe the breath and, each time you notice you've gone into thinking, simply return to the breath.
- Tune into your heart, and witness any emotion that arises—and how, given space, it moves and changes.

If boredom arises when a Sure Thing is on the horizon, I take a few minutes to meditate, either alone or with Bill. It's my sure-fire, wholesome way to shift boredom. What is yours? If you don't have one yet, play with one of the methods above—or experiment until you find your own. Just resist the mainstream impulse to stuff every quiet moment with noise and data.

Lastly, there may be times you're just not in the mood, because of changing hormonal levels, health challenges, or life circumstances. But even if you're not up to engaging with someone else, I encourage you to make the effort to connect with your inner lover, however briefly. You might wrap your arms around yourself in a loving hug. Or light some incense or a candle. Play a song you adore. Eat a piece of chocolate, putting your full attention on the taste as it melts on your tongue. Or choose any of the myriad ways you experience bodily pleasure. Engaging with your inner lover when you don't feel like it will grow your resolve and sweeten your relationship with this part of yourself.

⟡ Final Preparations ⟡

Collect the supplies you wish to have on hand. Just like an altar, this can be super simple or deliriously decadent. At a minimum, I suggest incorporating something to awaken at least one of your senses, along with a lubricant of your liking.

There is no right way to do this. Follow *your* bliss. Here are some suggestions for supplies:

- Your favorite scented oil, for anointing your and your partner's body. Or essential oil in a diffuser, or incense.
- Music that gets you in the mood.
- Finger foods to tantalize your taste buds or nibble off your partner's body.
- Silky fabric or feathers to caress your bodies.
- A flower arrangement to elevate your visual field.
- Sex toys for exploration and discovery.
- Candles.

Finally, set the space. Make sure the room is warmed to your liking. Place the lube, sex toys, and any sensory delights within arm's reach. You might try warming the lube by placing it in a jar of hot water. Then ask yourself or your beloved, "What would be most pleasurable right now?"

☆ Partner Practices to Get in the Mood ☆

In her book *Sex Talks,* Vanessa Marin explains what happens with brain chemistry early on in a love affair. "The neurotransmitters in your brain go buck wild... the dopamine levels mimic being high on cocaine. But this stage can last for only one to three years, max. At that point, your previously surging high-octane transmitters—serotonin, dopamine, and norepinephrine—get replaced with oxytocin and vasopressin, which are designed to help us relax and bond."[18]

Isn't that a relief? You can put to rest any fantasies that the level of turn-on you felt for your partner at the start of your relationship is supposed to last. No more wasting time thinking something's wrong with your relationship! Instead, you can put that energy toward discovering new ways to spark arousal and reach fulfillment.

Below are some possibilities to get you and your partner going. You can also use these to start your Sure Thing with a different kind of foreplay. As usual, follow your internal guidance and please~o~meter. And as always—if you're inspired, make up your own!

Retell Your Relationship Origin Story

Recount the story of when you first met, your first kiss, or the first time you made love. Describe when you first felt chemistry between the two of you. Or when you first saw each other naked. Or any memory from the early days of your relationship that fans your pheromonal fire. Remembering and reminiscing about your initial lusty connection can be a wonderfully arousing activity.

Let Music Move You

What songs do you immediately start to groove to? Put on those songs and move and dance in a way that turns *you* on as your partner watches. Feel the music and move your hips, your arms, your fingers, your head. Or you might dance with your partner. Bill and I often begin our Sure Thing with a dance. I love to rub and grind on him to a song with a sultry beat.

Chase that Tail

One of you chases the other. When Bill chases me, it turns me on and makes me giggle all at once. I let him catch me and then, if I can wriggle out of his grip, I slip away for more. Being chased is a gloriously freeing, primal, and playful activity.

The Two-Step[19]

This is a soothing and intimacy-engendering practice recommended by sex therapist Stephen Snyder in his book *Love Worth Making*:

Step 1: Spend time in bed together doing nothing in particular. Perhaps you talk for a bit—not necessarily about something erotic. At some point, begin to attune to your senses. Notice your breath, the feel of air on your skin, the press of your body against the mattress. Open to just being in the moment, in your body, lying in the bed. Eyes open or closed. Notice what arises.

Step 2: At some point in Step 1, arousal may enter the scene. Enjoy it! Stay with yourself and take the arousal ride—sometimes it may be subtle, sometimes not. Don't worry about your partner, let them take care of themselves. Eventually, you may want to tell your partner about your arousal and make a request for whatever it is you desire.

Snyder reminds us that "it's crucial when you go looking for erotic inspiration that you first look within yourself."[20]

Hugging Till Relaxed

Invented by David Schnarch, hugging till relaxed is an exceptional tool that reveals your level of differentiation. That is, your ability to be sovereign and independent, physically and emotionally, when you are close to others. Hugging till relaxed allows you to hold onto yourself while in close proximity to your partner. It can be a deliciously intimate experience on its own and can certainly lead to arousal.

"Hugging till relaxed," writes Schnarch, "is elegant and simple. The basics require four sentences: stand on your own two feet. Put your arms around your partner. Focus on *yourself*. Quiet yourself down—*way* down."[21]

Eye Gazing

Find a comfortable seat facing your partner with your knees touching. You can sit on a cushion, on a chair, or on a couch. Make sure you both can sustain the position without discomfort. Set a timer for 10, 20, or even 30 minutes.

Look into one another's eyes. At first, you may giggle, smile, or feel awkward. No problem. Let the giggles come up and out. Don't try to restrain a smile, though don't indulge it either. You may wish to allow your breath to synchronize—inhaling and exhaling together.

The practice of eye gazing cultivates the ability to be present in the present moment with another person. Remember, it's a practice. If you find yourself spacing out or fantasizing about getting naked with your partner, for the duration of this exercise, bring yourself back. You can use your breath as an anchor, or your partner's eyes, or any other means that will allow you to empty and open to the here and now.

Empty Presence

The next phase of eye gazing is Empty Presence, as described in the *Pleasure Fit for a God/dess* section of this chapter. In that section, you're looking into your own eyes—but here, you're looking into your beloved's. Everything else is exactly the same. Breathe slowly and deeply. Allow the normal coordinates of consciousness to dissolve as you enter into a more receptive and expansive state together.

Tantric Practices

Synchronized Circular Breathing

1. Sit facing one another in a comfortable position, close enough that your knees touch.
2. Place your right hand on your partner's heart. Have your partner place their right hand on your heart.
3. Place your left hand over your partner's hand on your heart. Have your partner do the same.
4. One of you inhales as the other exhales. Then exhales as the other inhales. This creates a circular breath.
5. Continue for as long as you'd like. Notice the effect of this practice on your mind, on your body, and on your connection with your partner.

Yab Yum

Initially, I recommend being partially clothed, or at least wearing something over the genitals, so it's less tempting to succumb to intercourse. It may be most enjoyable to have the larger bodied person be "partner 1" in this exercise.

1. Partner 1 sits upright and cross-legged. Use pillows and cushions to find a comfortable position. If that's not possible, sit on a chair or the edge of a bed.
2. Partner 2 sits on partner 1's lap, wrapping your legs around their waist and arms around their shoulders. Partner 2 can allow your legs to hang loosely if you're on a chair.

3. Partner 1 wraps their arms around partner 2's waist.

4. Breathe together, or inhale and exhale in a circular breath. Focus on different energy centers in the body as you breathe. Start at the crown, the top of the head. Move to the third eye, between the eyebrows. Then to the throat, heart, solar plexus, genitals, and the base of the spine. Or start at the base of the spine and move up to the crown. Or move intuitively between energy centers.

5. Rock back and forth. Observe where the energy moves. Play. Explore. Experiment.

Honor the Divine in Your Beloved

For those who want to embody the god or goddess you are, this is a fun one. Instead of exploring the divine within, you'll be acknowledging the divine in another.

One of you takes the role of god or goddess, and the other the role of adorer or devotee.

- The god or goddess stands in full glory, radiating the energy of love, compassion, sovereignty, strength, or whatever lights you up. If there is a deity you are drawn to, invoke them, call them in, embody them. Allow the overflowing energy to pour forth from your heart, hands, eyes, lips, tongue, and genitals.

- The devotee receives their partner as the god or goddess they are. Allow their radiance to move, awe, and open you. As you feel ready, honor them by fully prostrating before them, kissing their feet, bowing at their feet, or in whatever way you are moved to revere them.

- Switch roles. Bask in this mutual recognition of your divine nature.

⭐ Catalyze Passion with Closeness or Space ⭐

Creating a supportive, low-stress, and affectionate context is crucial for both partners. "Passion doesn't happen automatically in a long-term, monogamous relationship," writes Emily Nagoski. "Passion does happen as long as the couple takes deliberate control of the context. For some couples, that context feels like creating closeness. For others, it feels like creating space."[22]

Which context generates passion in your relationship? Do you feel hotter for your partner after you've spent the day together, or after you've spent some time apart?

If being together, intimately conversing, deepening trust, and maintaining close proximity feels more your style, plan for that before a Sure Thing. On the other hand, if distance creates the edge that sparks passion between you, take some space from one another before a Sure Thing. What is clear is that "couples who sustain a strong sexual connection over multiple decades have two things in common: they are friends who prioritize sex."[23]

I hope this chapter has shown you that there are an abundance of ways to prepare your mind and body for a Sure Thing. From the variety of warm-up exercises and explorations provided, may your imagination be sparked as you feel your way into discovering what's right for you. Attune to your please~o~meter as a foolproof guide. And just like the ever-changing nature of reality, so too will your appetite change for how you want to get primed and prepped for a Sure Thing.

Spread the Sure Thing Energy

"When you learn, teach. When you get, give."
—Maya Angelou

♥ Challenge

Make eye contact and smile at three strangers today, carrying the energy from your last Sure Thing into the world.

♥ Challenge Afterglow

How did you evoke the energy from your last Sure Thing so you could share it with a stranger? How was this for you? Did they respond? If yes, how?

Love Ripple Challenge Notes

Chapter 10
Resistance

The most radical act in a world that profits from our numbness is to feel.

Resistance can't always be shrugged off easily. Sometimes it feels like an inertia magnet, seducing me into inactivity, complacency, and disconnection. I have a few strategies that usually help, but what happens when they don't?

Some offer the "fake it till you make it" approach, which may work well in circumstances like a job interview or public speaking, but not so much in the bedroom. When it comes to pleasure and orgasm, there's already been far too much faking it, especially by women.

This chapter explores playful and effective ways of engaging resistance.

✩ Resistance in Real Time ✩

When I first sat down to write this chapter, my own resistance was thick. I procrastinated by returning emails and texts until I forced myself to open the manuscript. I felt a pit in my belly, and a general lethargy and malaise crept into my body. The thought "I don't wanna" echoed in my head.

Then I remembered: I have a ritual practice to encourage creative flow and motivate me to write this book. I wrote it when I first began, knowing I'd hit moments like this. I spoke the incantation below out loud:

I call in the Muse to delight, surprise, inspire, and guide me ~ Thank you!

Little e tumbles down from the golden place into my belly ~ Welcome! I love you!

Tingles abound as I open to the interconnected mycelium wisdom pathways beneath me, rooting me deeper into this body and this land. I give thanks and call on my ancestors to guide and support me. I give thanks to the Lisjan Ohlone ancestors of the land I live upon.

I open my crown and the light-sensitive, creative centers of my brain and connect with the crystalline web of light that connects all with all, the interdimensional web of consciousness.

I P-pump shakti up the spine, flowering open the heart. Radiant light bathes my pineal gland as energy cascades over the top of my head, down the front of my body, swirls up my back and around again and again and again.

Rooted and expanded, I open to receive.

I began the incantation, but something didn't feel right. I was just going through the motions. The energy wasn't moving in my body as it normally did.

Ugh. It's not working, I thought.

Before the resistance grew even stronger, I jumped up from my desk and started to shake. I sounded and sang and let it all out. The heaviness dissipated after a few minutes. I tried the incantation again. It felt right. The creative energy began to percolate, and I was ready to face this chapter.

For me, shaking and vocalizing often release resistance. Another strategy that supports me is accountability. My commitment to share this practice propels me when I don't want to write. It also helps that I've told people. The same can be true with your Sure Thing practice. Making a commitment to a weekly practice, and telling friends about it, can ease the struggle when resistance arises.

⭒ Playing with Resistance ⭒

While writing this book, I felt a strong desire to share the Sure Thing practice with others. I didn't want to wait until the book was published, so I created an online course. When I told a friend about it, she said, "If this were my rodeo, I'd have the course be as many weeks as chapters in the book. That way, you complete a chapter a week."

Ta-da! A course structure that would support me to finish the book was created.

During the class on resistance, I asked Sandy, one of the participants, to speak *as* her resistance. With an audible exhale, she agreed.

"I am your resistance," she began, "and you are not allowed to touch yourself. Your daughter is asleep in the next room. A good mother doesn't do that. A good girl doesn't do that. You have to find the right moment and the right space. You can't just go wild. Who do you think you are?"

"How was it to speak that out loud?" I asked.

"It feels dense. Like I'm being held down and caged in. Like there are chains locking me up."

"Whose voice is that?" I asked. "Whose thoughts are those?"

"I was raised in a Catholic family where there were a lot of restrictions and things forbidden, including the color red. Even though I've released so much, I feel like there's something really deep that's still there."

"Have you named this part of your inner pantheon? Is there an inner nun or priest in there?"

Her face closed. "I'm afraid to look at this dark Catholic part. I want to push it away."

"I understand," I said, gently. "And the truth is, this part is *already* seated at your consciousness roundtable."

Sandy nodded. "I don't want to say I hate this part, because it's too strong. But, I don't want it to be there."

"This *is* the resistance you've been experiencing," I told her. "This voice is inside of you. And you have a choice. You don't have to turn toward it, but it is there. You can engage with this part however you want. You could turn your back, slam the door, and try to shut this part out. Or you could be curious about it, perhaps ask some questions. Do you wear a habit or a collar? What is your favorite part of the Bible? What is your most urgent prayer?"

Sandy chuckled. "Yeah, I like that. I need to face this part. I should try to have a conversation with her and see what happens."

I assured Sandy that there were no *shoulds* or *have-tos*. I told her it was entirely up to her how she'd like to navigate it. But only when she leaned into it with openness would she discover what was in there. There may be a hidden treasure—but she would only find it if she gathered the courage and, at her own pace, got to know this part of her inner pantheon.

Once you acknowledge and get to know your inner resistors, they'll have less sway over you. Then, when you don't want them around, you can send them off on an outing. I imagine an inner nun would love to go to a chapel and pray for world peace. An inner stubborn teenager could be occupied for hours with TikTok or video games. An inner wounded kid could be sent off on an adventure with a magical babysitter.

Now, actually imagine one of *your* inner resistors being happily occupied. What does that feel like? Are you able to focus your attention on something else? As you become more familiar with the resistance within, possibilities for play abound.

When the resistance is too great and nothing will ease it, pause. Go to your altar, if you have one. Remember and reconnect with your intention to start a Sure Thing in the first place. Let that inspiration wash over you.

And if you're still not feeling it, no problem. How about just lying on your bed and breathing? Look around, touch the covers, stretch out your limbs, wriggle out tension. Notice anything you see or feel that is pleasurable—a color, a texture, an image, a certain stretch. And then just let it in.

✰ Stay True to You ✰

Your Sure Thing practice will reliably nourish both body and soul, as long as it's rooted in staying true to your desire and your body's signals.

♡ EXERCISE 13: Excavating Erotic Blocks & Accelerators ♡

First, read through the entire exercise a few times. Then enact it from memory. Do the best you can to recall the specifics of the exercise, but don't focus on getting it exactly right. You may wish to record the three questions and play them back. Allow yourself to surrender to your own inner knowing and guidance as you identify your erotic blocks and accelerators.

1. Take a deep breath and let your mind and energy settle. Use the 4-1-5 breath from page 6 or think "Open" on the inhale, "Empty" on the exhale.

2. Allow your awareness to drop like an anchor into your belly. Envision your consciousness settling and expanding, like a large, still lake.

3. As you hear or remember each of the questions, imagine a stone being dropped into the lake. Notice what shapes, images, or words appear on the surface of the water.

4. Question #1: What helps me enter into an erotic state of mind? Open and receive until you feel complete.

5. Clear your mind. Allow the lake to return to a crystal-clear, still reflection. Then drop the next question in and observe what happens.

6. Question #2: What beliefs, conditions, or inner states make it easy for me to say yes to pleasure? What am I doing and how do I feel when saying yes to pleasure is easy? Open and receive until you feel complete.

7. Clear your mind. Allow the lake to become a clear, still mirror. Then drop the next question in and observe what happens.

8. Question #3: What beliefs, conditions, or inner states make pleasure difficult or impossible to access? What am I doing and how do I feel when saying yes to pleasure is unimaginable? Open and receive until you feel complete.

Use the following journal page to capture what you're learning about your erotic blocks and accelerators in words or images.

My erotic blocks and
accelerators are...

On occasion, I've overrode what my pussy was trying to tell me during a Sure Thing. In those instances, it's not unusual for irritation to erupt in my urethra—it feels like the beginning of a urinary tract infection. It's as if my body is letting me know exactly what happens when I don't respect my own boundaries!

In Louise Hay's *You Can Heal Your Life*—a great resource that lists the likely emotional holding or reactivity associated with many physical ailments—she describes the cause of a urinary tract infection as "being pissed off." This generally feels true, in my case. I may have been pissed off at Bill for not adhering to my requests. Or at myself for overstepping my own boundaries.

If you find yourself crossing one of your boundaries or ignoring one of your blocks, please be gentle with yourself. Often, we don't know where a boundary is until we've crossed it. Now you know where that boundary is and you can set an intention to honor it in the future.

Remember, you're a pleasure researcher. Tap into your inner scientist as you excavate more of your erotic blocks and accelerators.

Herbal Remedies for Urethral Discomfort and Urinary Tract Infections

- If you're having an acute reaction, drink *a lot* of unsweetened cranberry juice. If I drink one 32-oz jar over a few hours, that will usually relieve any pain and clear the infection. I dilute the cranberry juice with room temperature or warm water. Be sure to buy it unsweetened, as sugar will only feed the infection. It's very tart and will likely make you pucker.

- If your yoni tends to become irritated from intercourse, I recommend regularly drinking hibiscus tea for its antimicrobial and anti-inflammatory properties, especially the day or two before vaginal penetration.

☆ Playing with Your Partner's Resistance ☆

Okay, so they don't wanna. Really? We'll see…

If your partner is resistant to a Sure Thing, give them full permission to be right where they are—and you focus on *you*. You may choose to practice a Solo Sure and let them know about it. Lo and behold, before too long, someone may join you in your pleasure explorations! But try to avoid expectations. Focus instead on fulfilling *your* Sure Thing intention.

Another thrilling option is seduction, with no strings attached. Invite your inner seductress out with some sultry music. Move in a way that feels good for you. This may lead to a striptease or perhaps a lap dance for your partner. Maybe a nibble on your partner's neck, a lick on their ear. Whatever feels playful and unconditional. Be as flirtatious as you dare, all the while respecting any boundaries they may have set.

The key is to be respectful of your partner and notice their body language. You might invite them to join you in one of the *Partner Practices to Get in the Mood* in Chapter 9. Or you could offer your partner a sensorium.

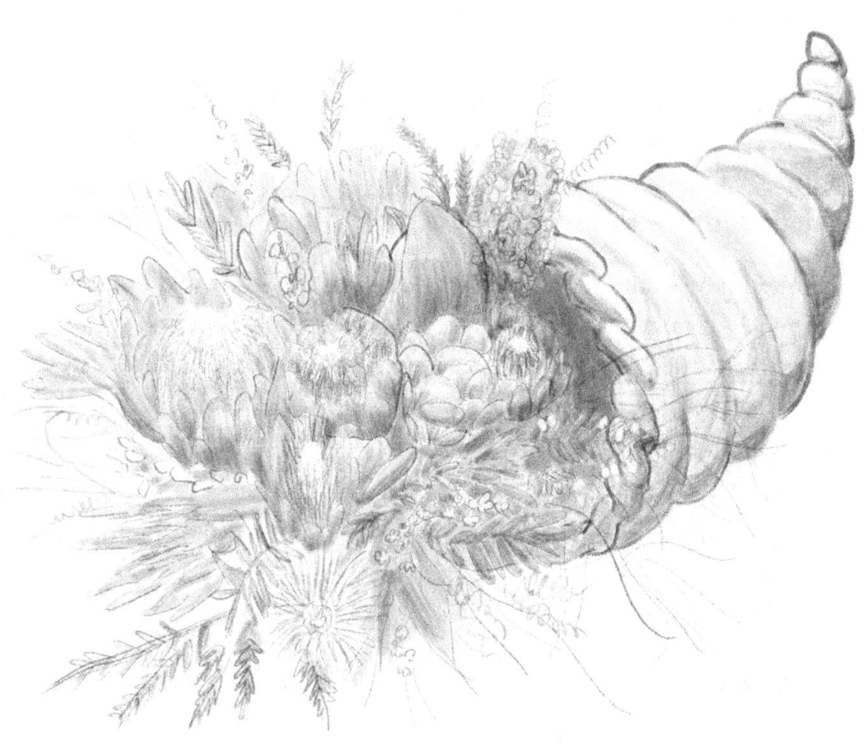

⭐ How to Create a Sensorium ⭐

A sensorium is just like it sounds: a feast for the senses. Gather at least one item to titillate each sense—except for the eyes, as you will blindfold your beloved. Beyond that, the possibilities are boundless. Here are some ideas to get your creative juices flowing:

- **Sense of Taste:** chocolate, honey, whipped cream, strawberries, banana, fresh mint leaves
- **Sense of Touch:** feathers, rose petals, faux fur, soft brushes, sandpaper, crystals, massage oil
- **Sense of Smell:** flower, essential oil, herbs (rosemary, sage, thyme), scented candle
- **Sense of Sound:** chimes, bell, rattle, musical instrument, gorgeous music

Blindfold your beloved and have them lie down on a soft rug, a bed, a massage table, or wherever they can absolutely relax and surrender. Make sure they are comfortable. Would they like a pillow under their knees? A blanket? Anything else?

You are now an ecstasy magician, about to take your beloved on a journey to ignite their senses.

While you'll be directing the experience, please revel in the pleasure as well. Perhaps do a few P-Pumps to begin. Then, you may wish to wash and massage your beloved's hands and/or feet. Have warm water, massage oil or lotion, and towels nearby.

Next, pick up a bite of food and gently wave it under their nose. Tantalize their taste buds by teasingly rolling it over their lips. Build the anticipation as much as you'd like. Whenever you're ready, reward them with a taste. As they chew, maybe you take a bite, too. Or maybe you pick up a feather and begin to caress them with it.

Then place a crystal in their hand as you hold an herb under their nose. Experiment with different combinations. Let your creativity and please~o~meter be your guide. Go wild with pleasure possibilities!

A sensorium can last as long as you'd like, and it can certainly transition into sexual play. It's best not to have an agenda or expectations. Follow the bliss you're co-creating. If you're both excited about the prospect of switching roles, go ahead—and notice which role you prefer.

⭐ Unpacking Resistance *Together* ⭐

If, after your most creative and whimsical invitations, your beloved is still a *no,* this may be the moment to gently remind them of the shared commitment you made to the practice. If not now, when? Agree to a specific day and time for your Sure Thing. Remember to tune into your goal. Generally, the goal of a shared Sure Thing is to deepen in intimacy and pleasure with your partner. If they're not feeling it, no problem, and no need to coerce them. Instead, you may want to take this opportunity to examine resistance together.

Invite your beloved into a conversation. If they resist, that could be a great opportunity to explore their resistance in real time. If they're not open to that, set aside a time on the calendar. Or, if it feels like you need more support, consider booking a session or two with a couple's therapist.

When the time is right, with tenderness and patience, ask your partner:

- What are you feeling in your body?
- What thoughts are you aware of?
- Is it okay if we stay here, breathe together, and see what happens?

Follow your intuition. Maybe ask them to speak as the resistance. Be gentle and encouraging. Move slowly.

Fill in the journal page below with words or images of you and your partner's experience of resistance.

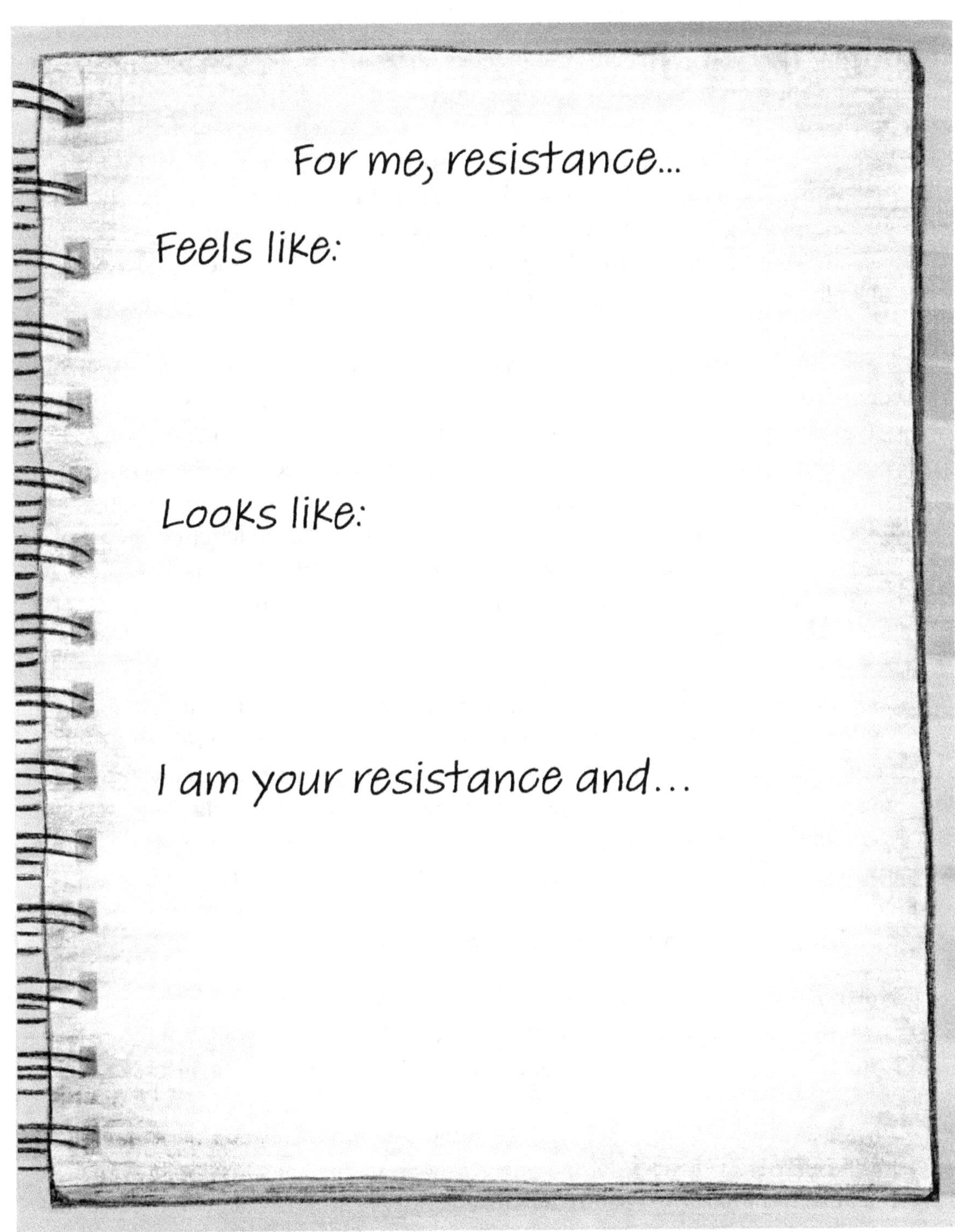

After some resistance exploration, check in with your partner. What are they aware of now? Has anything shifted? Has the resistance abated or increased?

It may take some effort to counter the apathy that resistance can conjure. Don't guilt-trip yourself or your partner. If your practice wanes for a week or two, take notice—is there an effect on you? Is there an effect on your relationship?

Recently, my beloved was exhausted. He simply didn't have the capacity for our Sure Thing. The second week, I noticed myself feeling edgier. My fuse was shorter. I watched myself get angry, blame him for my experience, and become a victim all in one fell swoop. Then I realized I could've had a Solo Sure when he wasn't available. After all, *I am responsible for my own pleasure.* And my unease lifted.

A Sure Thing is meant to catalyze whatever wants to come alive between you and your partner in the moment. I encourage you to do your best to release any expectations of what a Sure Thing is *supposed* to look like. Focus instead on how you feel. If you're feeling frustrated, angry, or contracted, let yourself feel it all the way through. For me, it helps to shake and shout when I have difficult emotions. Ideally, I do this alone, so no one else inadvertently picks up any residual yuck from my release. Discover what works for you to fully feel and then fully let go of emotions. Also, be mindful not to direct them at others. This is tricky and takes practice, patience, and a lot of self-compassion.

Once the difficult emotions have dissipated, have a heart-to-heart conversation with your partner. Return to your original intentions, those which catalyzed you to commit to a Sure Thing practice in the first place. Discern what is true now. If they no longer resonate, set new intentions. Recommit to whatever feels aligned and joyful. Remember, a Sure Thing practice will not always be easy. Sometimes it will test your growing edge; other times, it will call your relationship into greater depth.

⭐ Sure Thing Incantation: Call it In! ⭐

Earlier in this chapter, I shared the incantation I wrote to inspire me to complete this playbook. Now it's your turn to craft an incantation for your Sure Thing practice. Turn on your imagination. Crank open the floodgates of fantasy. Invite in the Muse.

What are the words, images, energies, and archetypes that arouse you? Are there specific entities or deities you find energizing or compelling? Maybe Aphrodite or Apollo? Eros or Shakti? What in the universe stirs your mind and body? What language gets you in the mood?

In the scroll below, write your very own Sure Thing incantation. You may want to invoke your wild sensual self or inner lover and have them write it.

You may want to read your incantation before each Sure Thing or plan to read it periodically to stay connected with your deeper intention. And should you need some oomph before your Sure Thing, read your incantation out loud. You now have your own personalized poetic pizzazz to call on at times when resistance arises.

Please know that your dance with resistance will ebb and flow. When you feel resistance, try to greet it—"I know you," or "Thought I'd ditched you forever… no such luck," or "Welcome back." The sooner you see it, the sooner you can address it. Resistance, in its own way, is a gift—it offers you an opportunity to lean into your commitment and devotion to deeper intimacy with yourself, your partner, and all that this practice represents. It may require some effort to face the resistance head-on, with your heart open. But remember, you already have all of the support you need within you. Plus, you have this playbook as your ally. You got this!

Great Mother Hug

"War must cease. We are all members of one big family; now is the time to eliminate fighting and contention. The world was created to be a thing of beauty. If there is no love between us, that will be the end of our home, the end of our country, and the end of our world. Love generates heat and light. That is the spirit of Aikidō training."

—Morihei Ueshiba, Founder of Aikidō

When I find myself around someone who is emotionally distraught, even if I don't know them well, I ask if they would like a hug. My offer is almost always accepted. I silently call in the Great Mother energy of nourishment, sanctuary, and unconditional love. Then I open my arms to the person in distress. Sometimes I imagine I'm a giant tree, deeply rooted, with branches reaching to the sky, offering unwavering support.

♥ Challenge

When you find yourself with someone experiencing difficult emotions, ask them if they'd like a hug. If they accept, invite the Great Mother (or any energy that feels unconditionally loving—for more on this go to *What is an Archetype?* on page xvii) into your heart, mind, and body. Feel yourself held in Her all-encompassing embrace as you open and receive this person into your arms. Relax. Surrender. Breathe.

Hold them until you feel them start to pull away. Give them a gentle squeeze to encourage them to stay in your embrace longer, if they'd like. As you separate, stay present and in your body.

💜 Challenge Afterglow

What did you experience? How did the other person respond? Would you do it again?

Chapter 11
Putting It All Together

Love always triumphs over hate, and it's much more pleasurable.

There are as many ways to practice the Sure Thing as there are shapes of snowflakes. This chapter includes some options to illustrate the wide range of possibilities. Also included are two journeys: the first is to your inner Temple of Love, the second is to meet your inner saboteur. In addition, there's a quick reference guide with a step-by-step Sure Thing map, and finally an exploration of likely obstacles.

To explore the plethora of options available for your Sure Thing, let's begin with your inner lover, as she is likely a font of fantasy, creativity, and turn-on.

Let's go on a journey to your inner Temple of Love. This type of internal adventure is most meaningful when the conscious mind is relaxed and the subconscious leads in a semi-dreamlike state. To surrender into this experience, you have options: you can have a friend guide you through the journey, you can record it on your phone and play it back, or you can read it through a couple of times and go from memory.

The "she/her" pronoun and female genitalia are used in this journey. Please change the words to reflect what feels right to you.

♡ GUIDED VISUALIZATION to Your Temple of Love ♡

- Please use one of the previous practices in this playbook (or one of your own) to relax fully into this moment. Feel the support of the earth underneath you whether you are lying down or sitting. Exhale deeply and let go.

- Direct your awareness to settle in your belly. Take a few slow, deep breaths.

- Place one hand on your heart and the other on your pussy or belly. Breathe. Soften. Open.

- Invite your inner lover to reveal herself. Be patient. Allow her to make an entrance or perhaps she invites you into her boudoir.

- Once you sense the connection with your inner lover, take note of how you feel and what you perceive.

- Then, your inner lover reaches out and takes your hand. She leads you into her Temple of Love. Notice the lushness. Open to the scents, the sounds, the decadence.

- What do you see? Is there an altar? Are you indoors or out in nature? Which colors do you observe? Are there flowers? Plants? Flowering vines? A canopy of trees? A lake? A pool? A hot tub? A bed of leaves or pillows? What images do you see? Is this temple lit by natural light, candlelight, a fire burning brightly in a fireplace? Take in the details of the space as best you can.

- How do you feel being in this Temple of Love?

- Then, you notice your inner lover begins to move. You realize she's communicating some of the ways she'd like to practice a Sure Thing. It's as if you're watching an erotic movie. You observe her practicing a solo Sure Thing. Perhaps she's also practicing with a partner, and even multiple partners.

- Allow your inner lover to express herself fully. Let her go wild. Let her show you all of her fantasies. You simply witness.

- How does she want to explore pleasure?

- How does she want to explore intimacy?

- How does she want to connect with you?

- Luxuriate in the Temple of Love with your inner lover. Spend as much time there as you wish.

- When you are replete and satisfied, thank your inner lover. Feel that you have one hand on your heart and the other on your pussy or belly. Bring your attention to your physical body. When you are ready, gently open your eyes.

In the following journal page, capture the highlights from the visit to your inner Temple of Love.

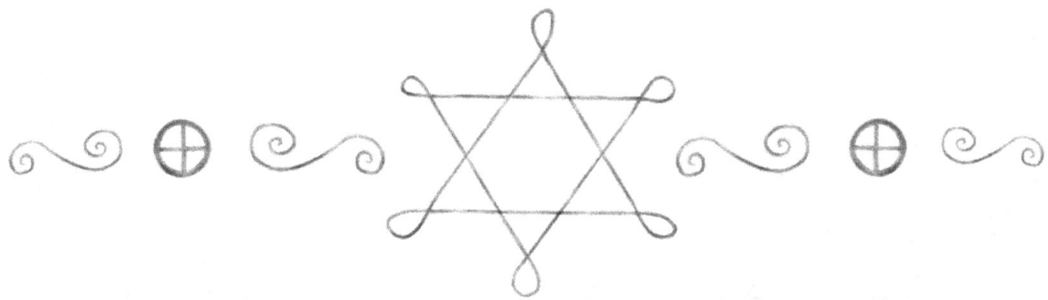

My visit to the Temple of Love

Now, in the scroll below, list some of the ways you'd like to practice a Sure Thing. Be sure to include any of your inner lover's fantasies that turn you on too! Continue to add to this list as you're inspired.

⭐ The Options Are Infinite ⭐

Below are some of the countless ways to practice a Sure Thing.

- **Slow, sensual dancing, either clothed, partially clothed, or naked.** Titillate yourself or your partner with the way you move your body. Turn on music that really does it for you and sensuously remove each item of clothing. And/or get down on all fours and undulate over to your partner, or to yourself in a mirror. Be a tease with a flash of tits and ass. Nibble, lick, rub, grind, whatever gives you the most pleasure. Stand up and intertwine your bodies in all different contortions, moving to the rhythm of the music and your inner please~o~meter.

- **The basic DO (Deliberate Orgasm) Date.** Ask your partner for a DO date. Get naked from the waist down or go full monty. Lie down with your legs splayed open. You may want a pillow under each knee. Have your partner get your favorite lube and get comfortable, either lying down next to you or sitting up next to you—perhaps having one leg over your torso and another under your knees. Experiment with different positions and find one where you are both comfortable. Use pillows and cushions for support. Your partner gets ample lube on his index finger and begins to stroke. Ask for exactly what you want—faster/slower stroke, different spot, firmer/lighter stroke, finger inside anus/pussy, etc. Remember, you are going for what feels the most pleasurable. Your goal is to experience ecstasy in the body and share this with a beloved. No agenda of climaxing or not climaxing. You may want to look into your beloved's eyes. Or your eyes may be closed. Or maybe a bit of both. Most importantly, whether you are the DOer or the DOee, try to feel every stroke. For more instructions on DO dates, go to the *Resources* section.

- **Mutual masturbation.** Eyes closed, eyes open, a little of both. This is oh so satisfying.

- **Masturbate as your partner watches.** It was edgy the first time I stroked myself as Bill watched. Our intimacy took a huge leap that day. How long does it take until your partner wants to join in? Your choice if you'd like to include them or if you'd prefer to continue to pleasure yourself.

- **Mutually masturbate you *and* your beloved.** This is a fun way to fully take charge. Begin by stroking yourself or your beloved. Then, lube up the other hand and get busy. Play with different rhythms and paces. Bring yourself to the edge. Pause. Bring your beloved to the edge. Switch hands. Get more lube. Attune to your please~o~meter.

♥ **Oral sex as a sensual feast.** One at a time or simultaneously, or a bit of both. Remember, a Sure Thing is not a tit for tat exchange. If your partner gives you oral sex, there's no obligation for you to return the favor. Each beloved is in their own sovereignty—full self-authority. Make choices from that place. This is not transactional, this is connecting sexually. Agree to what feels good and turns you on. Know you can change your mind at any moment. Attune to your please~o~meter and let that be your guide. *She Comes First* by Ian Kerner is an excellent step-by-step manual for cunnilingus exploration.

♥ **Intercourse, of course.** Anal, vaginal, or maybe both. Try a new position. Explore. Experiment. Take a risk.

♥ **Awaken your beloved** with a kiss, lick, or stroke on an erogenous zone.

♥ **Erogenous zone massage** for the breasts, nipples, labia, buttocks, cock, scrotum, or wherever you're feeling most turned on. Use oil if that'd bring more pleasure. Massage with hands, feet, tongue, teeth, breasts, cock. Make it up as you go.

♥ **Anoint** yourself or your beloved with holy oils.

♥ **Sensuous soak** in a bath or hot tub together.

♥ **Role-play** one of your erotic fantasies.

Create anew with each practice or repeat something you've already done. Even if you've done it before, it certainly won't be the same. Be in the moment, respond to what feels good to you, and ask for what you want.

Sometimes our Sure Thing is a quickie and sometimes we have hours of sensual research. For the years we've had a Sure Thing practice, there has never been an occasion when we weren't glad we practiced. Most weeks, we revel in how wonderful this practice is and end our session with a playful high five or fist bump.

⭐ Sure Thing Quick Reference Guide ⭐

Whether you practice solo or with a partner, this section brings everything together with step-by-step instructions covering both preparation for and the Sure Thing itself.

Step 1: Set a Sure Thing Intention
Why do you want to have a weekly Sure Thing? What is your underlying motivation? Set a simple and clear intention. When you read the intention, if you respond with "I definitely want that!" and it gives you a zing, you've found the right one.

To clarify an intention that thrills you, check out the *Setting an Intention* section in Chapter 7. If you're practicing with a partner, you may each have your own intentions, or you may share one. Go with what feels good and right and rousing to you.

Step 2: Create an Altar or Image that Evokes Your Intention

A physical representation of your Sure Thing intention will activate your practice. Make sure it's in a place where you'll see it often. It can be any piece of art that turns you on and reflects your Sure Thing intention. If it sounds like fun, create an altar (and put the image on it) to simultaneously amplify and magnetize your intention. Check out "Altar Creation" in the *Resources* section for more on this.

Step 3: Schedule Your Sure Thing

Whether practicing solo or with a partner, get it in your calendar. By having time allocated, you are tangibly prioritizing pleasure. Be sure to include time to prepare yourself and your space to guarantee fulfillment.

Step 4: Set Your Space

The scheduled time is approaching. Make sure your space is exactly as you want it. You may want flowers, chocolate, candlelight, music. If you like it tidy and clean, make it so. Be sure the temperature is just right. Space heaters can be helpful. And, make sure you have your favorite lube easily accessible.

Step 5: Prepare Yourself

What would help you relax, open, and soften in anticipation of your Sure Thing? A bath, a snuggle, a dance, a massage? Chapter 9 is chock-full of ways to get ready on your own and with a partner.

Step 6: Resistance? Let's Play!

Turn toward any resistance. Don't resist it. Say hello and then gently take the mic from your inner resistor and give it to your inner lover. If resistance persists, refer to Chapter 10.

Step 7: Let's Get It On

Begin with the question, "What would be most pleasurable right now?" If practicing solo, once you identify what it is, give it to yourself in a beautiful act of self-love. If practicing with a partner, one of you asks and the other answers. Be bold, generous, and stay true to you. Remember, with every request there are three responses: yes, no, and counteroffer.

Continue to follow your please~o~meter to determine what it is you want. Your desire may change. Pause or have your partner pause so you can re-attune to yourself to discern what it is you want now. Then, ask for it.

Ask. Surrender. Open. Receive. Pause to discern your desire. Repeat until replete.

Step 8: Plant the Seed for Your Next Sure Thing
In the afterglow, imagine your next practice. When will it be? Take note of any visions or desires. Seed the arousal and anticipation for your next Sure Thing so it grows throughout the week.

⭐ Identify Obstacles to Ensure Satisfaction ⭐

You have traversed most of the terrain in this playbook. You know yourself more intimately. Now's your chance to be honest about what specific blocks you can anticipate from your inner saboteur. Equipped with this list of plausible impediments, should one of them arise, it can be seen for what it is: a distraction from creating more connection, intimacy, and pleasure.

💗 GUIDED VISUALIZATION 💗

Oh, the Shenanigans of My Inner Saboteur

This type of internal adventure is most meaningful when the conscious mind is relaxed and the subconscious leads in a semi-dreamlike state. To surrender into this experience, you have options: you can have a friend guide you through the journey, you can record it on your phone and play it back, or you can read it through a couple of times and go from memory.

1. Settle and center yourself with the 4-1-5 breath from page 6 or engage in another calming practice.

2. In your mind's eye, imagine yourself resting comfortably against a giant old-growth redwood tree. Feel the firm, craggy bark on your back as you relax further. Sense the deep roots of the tree. Envision yourself feeling supported and grounded.

3. Let come to mind examples of you getting in your own way. Instances where you sabotaged yourself. Occasions where you blocked your success, talked yourself out of something you wanted, made excuses to justify inaction, or simply didn't do what you set out to do. Allow those memories to come into your mind.

4. Then, allow your inner saboteur to reveal themself more clearly. Don't worry about remembering everything. The aim here is to observe and get to know your inner saboteur.

  - Procrastination—How do you procrastinate? Recall an experience of procrastination.
  - Impatience—What causes you to be impatient? How do you react?
  - Doubt—When do you second-guess yourself? What is the effect of your self-doubt?
  - Self-criticism—Which self-critical thoughts cycle regularly through your mind? What provokes these thoughts?
  - Perfectionism—How does perfectionism show up in your life? What is its outcome?

5. Notice any patterns. Allow connections to form.

6. Now, invite your inner saboteur to come out of the shadows and fully show themself.

7. Once they do, ask your inner saboteur what it is they want. Receive them with as much openness and equanimity as possible. Spend as much time as you'd like getting acquainted.

8. When you feel complete for now with your inner saboteur, return to the image of you resting against the redwood tree. Breathe deeply. Integrate what you experienced.

You've seen some of the mischievous behaviors your inner saboteur uses to try to undermine you. Use the journal page to list the probable obstacles that may try to prevent you from following through on your Sure Thing practice.

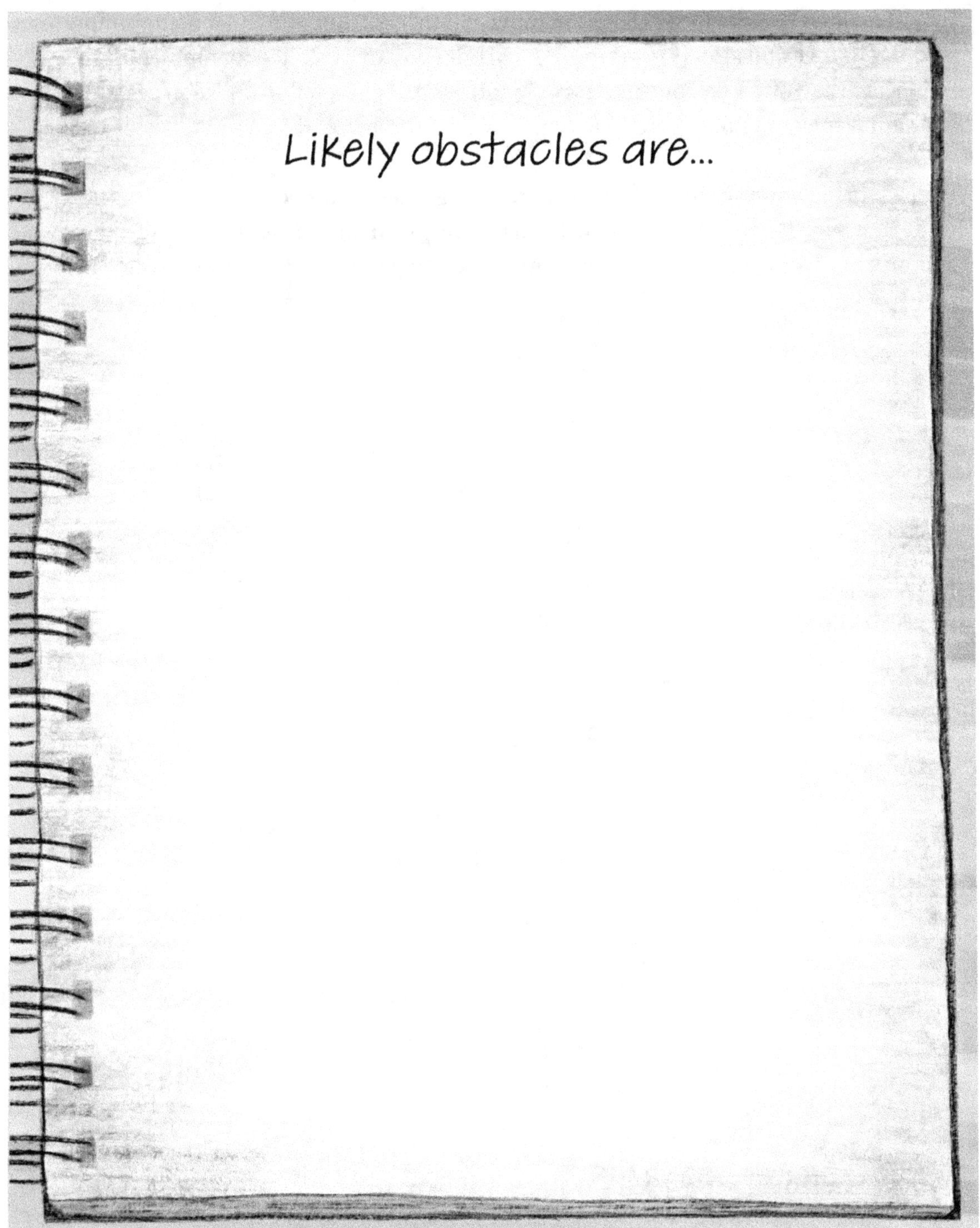
Likely obstacles are...

Just like all of the characters in your inner pantheon, your inner saboteur simply wants your love and attention. These parts of our ego can be skilled manipulators and seducers. They often use our inner kid mantra (i.e., "I'm a failure," "I don't matter," "I'm unlovable") to lull us into inaction. Don't fall for it.

Instead, bring your attention to your Sure Thing intention. Focus on what it is you want. The Sure Thing is a practice that will not only bring more pleasure, connection, and intimacy into your life, it will encourage you to passionately befriend yourself.

Drop the Reactivity and Respond with Love

"Love is the only force capable of transforming an enemy into a friend."
—Dr. Martin Luther King, Jr.

As you love yourself into wholeness by accepting the different parts of you, take that inclusive embrace into the world.

♥ Challenge

When you find yourself in a conflict with someone else, try to respond with an open heart and curiosity. Begin with a question, "Did you know…?" Asking a question is a wonderful way to de-escalate and open pathways of connection. Find a way, while being authentic and true to yourself, to bridge the divide with love.

♥ Challenge Afterglow

Were you able to bridge the divide? De-escalate the situation? If yes, how did you do it? If not, what would you do differently next time? What did you learn?

Love Ripple Challenge Notes

A Beginning Disguised As An Ending

*"Love never dies a natural death. It dies because we don't know
how to replenish its source."*
—Anaïs Nin

With this playbook in your hands, you now have a personalized path to replenishing love in your life. Whether you want to fall more deeply in love with yourself, reignite the blaze of passion with your partner, or simply expand your access to the infinite realm of pleasure, you have a map to all of that—and more.

Consider yourself at a crossroads. Congratulations! You made it here, my friend. Now, I invite you to join me on one final journey.

This type of internal adventure is most meaningful when the conscious mind is relaxed, so you can let the subconscious lead in a semi-dreamlike state. To surrender into this experience, you have options: you can have a friend guide you through the journey, you can record it on your phone and play it back, or you can read it through a couple of times and practice from memory.

♥ GUIDED VISUALIZATION : At the Crossroads ♥

- Get into a comfortable position. You may want to lie down.

- Please use one of the previous practices in this playbook (or one of your own) to bring yourself as much as possible into this moment.

- Close your eyes and feel the support of the earth underneath you as you invite your body to relax and surrender.

- Bring your full attention to the palm of your hand. Then place your palm on the top of your head. Slowly move your hand and your attention down your body until it rests on your belly. Invite the anchor of your awareness to drop deeper into your belly, noticing any sensations.

- Keeping the connection to your belly, let your awareness expand as wide as it will go. Perhaps that's just outside your body, perhaps it's as big as the room, perhaps it feels boundless.

- From here, invite any energies from our journey thus far to enter the space. As you feel ready, look around and notice who is here from your inner pantheon. Is your inner kid nearby? What about your wild sensual self? Your inner lover? Any other characters you're aware of from your inner pantheon?

- Are there any parts of you that aren't here yet—parts you'd like to have with you on this leg of the journey? If yes, please invite them now.

- Envision yourself, along with your inner posse, at a crossroads with two paths. You have a choice to make. Which path will you take?

- First, imagine you choose *not* to start a weekly Sure Thing practice. What does your life feel like in 1 month, 6 months, a year? How is your relationship with yourself? How is your relationship with your beloved? Steep in the vision of what your life might look like in the coming weeks, months, and years without this practice.

- Notice: Who is prominent in your inner pantheon without this weekly practice? Who has the mic? Which characters from your inner pantheon are at their side? Who *doesn't* get the mic, or is watching from the sidelines or shadows?

- Allow this vision to unfold in as much detail as possible. When you feel complete, take a few deep breaths, perhaps shake your limbs a little to let it go, and…

- Return. In your mind's eye, see yourself back at the crossroads: clear, present, and grounded.

- Now imagine you take the other path, the one where you *do* choose to commit to a weekly Sure Thing practice. What does your life feel like in 1 month, 6 months, a year? How is your relationship with yourself? How is your relationship with your beloved? Steep in the vision of what your life might look like in the coming weeks, months, and years.

- Who is prominent in your inner pantheon as you choose to practice a Sure Thing? Who has the mic? Who from your inner pantheon is hanging out with them? Who *doesn't* have the mic, or is watching from the sidelines?

- Allow this vision to unfold in as much detail as possible. When you feel complete, take a few deep breaths, let it go, and…

- Return. In your mind's eye, see yourself back at the crossroads: clear, present, and grounded.

- As you stand there, knowing what each path has in store for you, in which direction are you drawn? Which road feels right?

- Notice how you feel—notice any emotions or body sensations arising.

- Gently bring your attention to your breath. Feel your hand on your belly. In your own time, open your eyes.

Use the following journal page to take notes or draw about your experience at the crossroads.

At the Crossroads

Remember: You are 100% responsible for your pleasure. It's really as simple as that. Make a conscious choice based on your desire and what is true for *you*. Know that you have everything you need to succeed.

⭐ A Few Reminders ⭐

As with any enduring practice, a Sure Thing requires commitment, effort, and devotion.

Commitment is the key that unlocks the portal to your sensual and sexual fulfillment. The effort required to maintain your practice will pale beside the delights it brings. Devotion to your Sure Thing practice is a form of devotion to life itself—and life will respond with miracles.

"How?" you might ask. Because this practice fills you until you overflow. It awakens your creative power, since the seeds of creativity spring from our sexual centers. And it activates your self-empowerment—the deep knowing that you are the source of your own joy and fulfillment.

If you or your partner is feeling resistant, return to Chapter 10. Sit at your altar and listen to your inner guidance. Trust that you can meet and move through the lethargy, the blocks, the disempowering thoughts—whatever arises. Turn toward your inner resistor and send them to a protest or a punk show so you can get on with your Sure Thing practice.

Finally, I encourage you to continue to welcome and get acquainted with all of the personas in your inner pantheon. The more intimate you are with these aspects of self, the more quickly you can identify who has the mic. And then the more quickly you can return to a place of equanimity and *choose* who you want holding the mic. It's a game, and a lifelong one. A game that's impossible to lose so long as you stay curious and compassionate with yourself.

⭐ Radical Self Love ⭐

In *Mating in Captivity*, Esther Perel writes: "Complaining of sexual boredom is easy and conventional. Nurturing eroticism in the home is an act of open defiance."[24]

Your choice to start a Sure Thing practice is an act of defiance. It stands in the face of the social, cultural, and religious conditioning that has severed us from our innate sensuality. Initiating a Sure Thing practice is a reclamation of your body as a temple.

A Sure Thing practice is a declaration of sexual sovereignty, and in this culture, it is a radical act of self-love.

Here comes one final invitation to deepen your ongoing love affair with yourself:

Envision yourself as already fulfilled, no matter the particular circumstances of your life. You love yourself unconditionally. Take your time here, breathing into it, noting how the heart feels, how the body feels, what may be happening in the mind. Now, from this fullness: What promises or commitments do you wish to make with yourself?

You may want to include the voices of your inner kid and your inner lover as you complete the Heart Contract below.

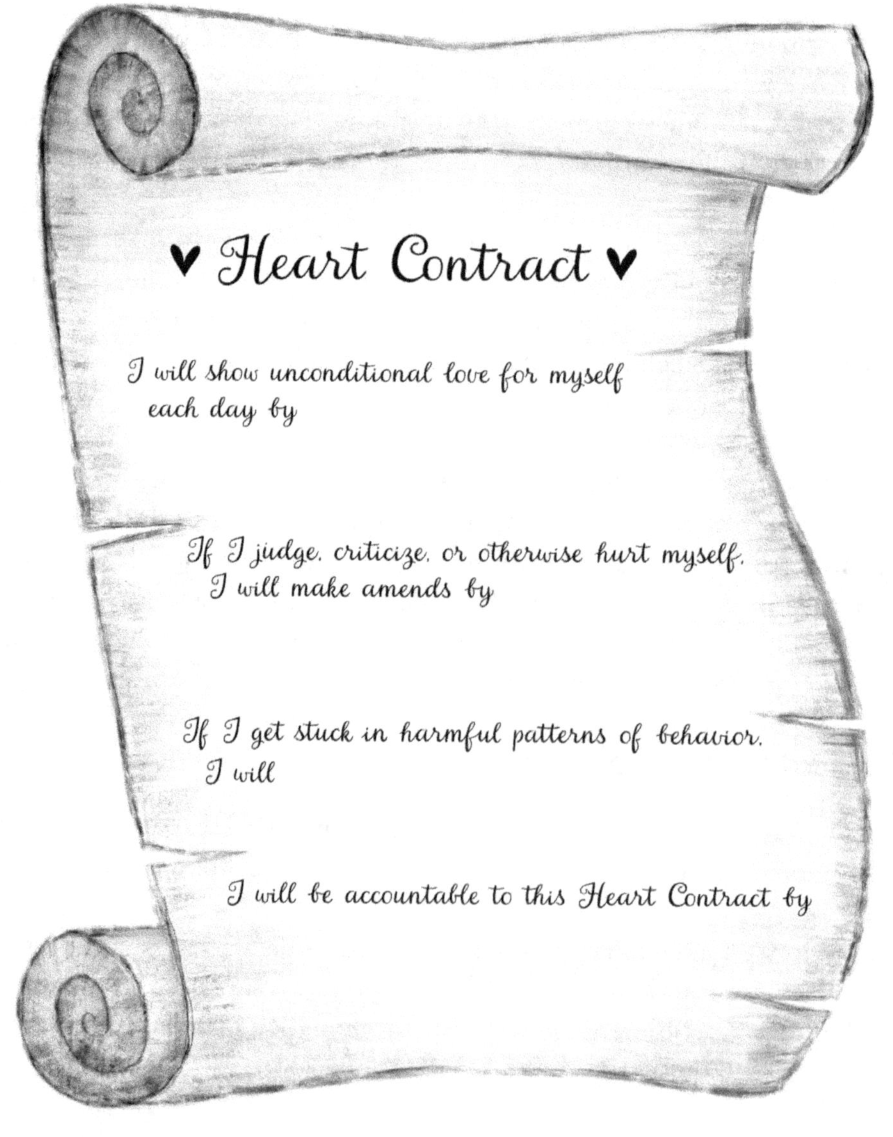

And if you'd like to make a heart contract with your beloved, just change the language in the scroll from "myself" to "my beloved."

⭐ What's Next? ⭐

The movement to bring more connection and love into the world is growing, and you are part of it! Each time you choose curiosity and openness over reactivity and judgment, you expand the wave. Each time you practice a Sure Thing, you contribute to the shift. Each time you respond to your own and others' foibles with compassion instead of criticism, you advance the game.

Intimacy is medicine for the heart and soul. And those who cultivate sexual pleasure aren't just more fulfilled—they tend to live longer, healthier lives. Studies show that people with satisfying sex lives tend to have lower rates of chronic disease, better heart health, stronger immunity, and improved mental well-being.[25] In addition, one large study[26] found that adults having sex weekly were nearly 50% less likely to die from any cause, including cancer, than those with infrequent sexual activity. Just in case you needed another reason to start a Sure Thing practice!

⭐ Be the Change ⭐

As your inner pleasure activist gets filled up, I encourage you to find a place to contribute that overflow to the world. There are many easy ways to do this. The first few listed below are about being a conscious consumer. In a capitalist society, purchasing products most aligned with your values is a marvelous way to take 100% responsibility for your consumption.

- There are many apps to support conscious consumption. Here are a few to consider:
  - *Ethical Barcode:* reveals what you're supporting if you purchase a particular product
  - *Boycat:* identifies and boycotts brands that conflict with your ethical values
  - *EWG's Healthy Living:* helps consumers identify healthier and safer products
- Most fast fashion items are made by people who are underpaid, overworked, and laboring in unsafe environments. You can help end the sweatshop crisis by choosing ethical brands, buying vintage or secondhand clothing, and organizing clothing swaps in your community.

- Single-use tampons and pads create millions of tons of plastic waste annually. They take 500-800 years to decompose, accumulating in landfills, and contributing to plastic pollution. Instead, here are some eco-friendly and economical options:
    - Sea Pearls are completely natural sea sponges that come from the ocean. These were my favorite! Be sure to match the size of the sponge with the heaviness of your flow. When full, wash the sponge in running water, then reinsert.
    - Menstrual cups are made from medical-grade silicone or rubber and collect menstrual fluid rather than absorbing it. They can be worn for up to 12 hours and reused after being rinsed and sterilized.

- Buy seasonal, locally produced food whenever possible. Find a nearby farmers' market and directly support those who grow your food. Cut out the middleman and reduce the carbon footprint of the food you eat.

- It's miraculous to turn on a faucet and have potable water pour forth! Do you know where your water comes from? If not, find out. You may be surprised. As you know, water is a precious resource and not wasting water is one way of honoring it. In the U.S., leaks waste approximately 1 trillion gallons of water annually and ten percent of homes have leaks that waste 90 gallons or more per day. To test for water leaks, perform a water meter test by turning off all water and watching for meter movement over an hour or two; if it changes, a leak exists. Go online for assistance or call a plumber.

- Learn about the original human inhabitants of the land you live upon. Do they have any surviving ancestors? Are there any established paths to make reparations? If so, consider contributing money or time to supporting these. When I looked into this, I learned that the Chochenyo-speaking Ohlone people were the first to steward the land that I'm blessed to live upon, known to them as Huchiun. Indigenous urban women founded the Sogorea Té Land Trust to rematriate the land. Sogorea Té created the Shuumi Land Tax, a voluntary annual contribution that non-Indigenous people can make to support their work and serve as a gesture of repair. If you live in the San Francisco Bay Area or want to learn more, visit www.sogoreate-landtrust.org/shuumi-land-tax/.

If none of these do it for you, find something that does. With the overflow generated by your Sure Thing practice, you may want somewhere beyond your immediate circle to channel it. What better way to share the surplus than to find a cause you're passionate about—one that contributes to a culture of kindness, justice, generosity, and love?

☆ The Sure Thing Love Experiment ☆

There are many ways to plug into The Sure Thing Love Experiment. For our latest offerings and to join the email list, go to www.surethingexperiment.com. Follow us on Instagram at **@elana.auerbach** and Facebook at **tinyurl.com/FBElana.**

Powered by pleasure, and with connection and love as our guiding lights, everything is possible!

Dedicated Blessing

May you experience more fulfillment than you ever thought possible. May that energy seep into all your relationships, surrounding you with ever more harmony, joy, and compassion. May your practice quicken humanity's awakening to the interconnectedness of all life, so that all beings may live in peace. May it be so!

Resources

In this section, you will find...

- Guidance to create an altar that inspires and delights you;
- Essential items to make your Sure Thing practice even more luscious;
- Deliberate Orgasm (DO) Date instructions; and
- A list of recommended reading.

☆ Altar Creation ☆

Creating an altar is a mighty and fun way to manifest your dreams. An altar functions as a focal point of magic, intention, and creative power. An altar is also a physical manifestation of the dreams and visions you'd like to actualize. An altar is evocative. It should affect, touch, and move you when you see it, sit with it, pray with it.

First, set a playdate with yourself to create your altar and add it to your calendar. If you're creating an altar with your Sure Thing partner, set an altar creation playdate together.

Step 1: Begin with Your Intention

If you don't have a clear and simple intention for starting a Sure Thing practice, find suggestions and direction in the *Setting an Intention* section in Chapter 7.

If you're excited about your intention, get it out so you can look at it. You may have written it in this playbook in Chapter 7 or Chapter 9, or in another journal you've been using for this adventure. And if your intention is in the form of an image, put it where you can see it.

Allow the words and/or image of your intention to infuse your consciousness. In your mind's eye, imagine the manifestation of your intention. Invite into your body the visceral experience of what your intention actualized feels like. Envision your intention coming to fruition in as much detail as possible. What do you feel in your body? In your heart? How is your relationship with yourself? With your beloved? How does realizing your Sure Thing intention affect other areas of your life?

As you bask in this vision of fulfillment, ask yourself:

What colors evoke this feeling in me? With which colors do I experience the realization of my intention?

- My intention is to deepen in intimacy, pleasure, and connection with myself and with Bill. The colors that evoke this feeling in me are deep red, pale pink, and fuchsia.
- Enter *your* response in the following journal page.

Which objects elicit your intention?

- For me, some of the objects are candlelight, flowers, sensual images of lovemaking, photos of me and Bill that soften my heart and turn me on, and essential oils (particularly Rosa Mystica and Ylang Ylang).
- Enter *your* response in the following journal page.

Are there symbols that you envision on your altar?

- The spiral and the vesica pisces really do it for me.
- Draw the symbols that evoke your intention in the following journal page.

My Sure Thing altar includes...

Step 2: Location, Location, Location

Now that you know some of what you want on your altar, choose a place for your altar to be. Make sure it's in a place where you'll see it often so it can be a reminder and inspiration for your Sure Thing practice. Your altar could be on your nightstand or on a dresser in your bedroom. You can use part of a bookshelf, a mantle, or the top of any flat piece of furniture. If you have an accessible garden, you may want to create an altar outside. If there's no obvious place for your altar, get a TV tray or other small table and put it where you'd like your altar to be.

Step 3: Vision into Form

Find an altar cloth or two in the colors you identified in Step 1. The altar cloth could be a scarf, a piece of fabric, a pillowcase, a tablecloth, a sheet, a rug, etc. The altar cloth serves as a canvas for your altar. Drape the altar cloth over whatever you'll be creating your altar on. You could even create a vertical altar and pin the altar cloth to a wall with push pins.

Remember, we are bringing formlessness—your intention, dream, wish—into form.

Which objects evoke the fulfillment of your dream? What symbolizes the manifestation of your intention? These can be from the natural world, statues or images of deities, photographs, paintings, the written word, a vase of flowers, a candle, crystals, etc., and any combination.

Choose a few and arrange them on top of the altar cloth—design for delight and whimsy. Objects may come and go from your altar as you're inclined. Your altar can be as simple or as extravagant as you'd like.

Once the altar is created, take a step back and take it in. How do you feel?

- If you feel excited, if energy is flowing, and you are lit up, congratulations! You've created your first Sure Thing altar.
- If you don't, what's missing? Review Steps 1, 2, and 3.

The altar serves as a reminder and magnet for your intention. Create your altar in a way that draws you to it, where you want to come close and commune with it.

Your altar can be as simple as an altar cloth and a candle, so long as it's infused with your intention and inspires *you*.

⭐ The Essentials ⭐

This section includes what I like to have at my fingertips before I begin a Sure Thing practice. Take this as a starter guide and add to it as you discover what *your* essentials are.

Space Setting

Create a sumptuous space where you'll be practicing your Sure Thing. The space may be as simple or ornate as you'd like. Remember, this is your practice; you get to design every bit of it exactly as you want it. Pillows are useful to prop up different body parts and ensure comfort. For some Sure Things, you may want to create a decadent space. Other times, your Sure Thing may happen in the middle of the night or be a quickie of some sort.

Lubricate the Love

Honestly, the only true essential for me is lubricant. Like most things, I was a late bloomer with lube, too. In my late 20s, during my first marriage, a friend shared about sex with her spouse and happened to mention lube.

"What? What's that?" I asked.

"Lube, you know, lubrication to make having sex that much more pleasurable and easeful," she answered.

I was intrigued and began experimenting with different lubes. My favorite is Yoni Flower Butter salve, handmade from wild herbs and other luscious (and edible!) ingredients from the Garden of Eden Apothecary.
www.gardenofedenapothecary.com

I have tried a lot of lubes for him and my favorite is good old coconut oil. It melts easily, it smells and tastes great, and it keeps everything smooth and flowing.

I keep a container of Yoni Flower Butter and coconut oil in my bedside table so they are easily accessible. I also keep a small container of each in my toiletry bag, so when I'm away from home, I have the essential ingredient for a spontaneous or regularly scheduled Sure Thing.

Try heating up the lube to add warmth to your sensuous exploration. And be sure to check the ingredients in your lube. Ideally, use lube that's edible and at a minimum has no parabens or other toxins.

In addition to keeping lube at arm's reach, I recommend keeping small towels or washcloths nearby, perhaps in your bedside table. After a juicy Sure Thing, it's lovely to roll over and get a towel without having to leave the bed.

Soundscape

Experiment with the soundtrack you'd like to accompany your Sure Thing. Bill and I have a fondness for music by the band Air when we're getting sexy together. We also created a playlist[27] with dance tunes for those Sure Things that start with a sensual dance party.

You may want to sing to each other, play Tibetan bowls, solfeggio tones to raise the frequency, or maybe a track with birdsong, a thunderstorm, or the ocean. Try different music, sound, and song to find what aurally opens your heart and gets you in the mood.

Temperature

For me, being cold is a big turn-off. Make sure the room where you'll be practicing your Sure Thing is nice and cozy. If there's a fireplace, spark it up. If you have a space heater, turn it on. And an easy way to heat things up between the sheets is a hot water bottle or two. If you don't have a simple way to heat up your space, find one. For those living in the San Francisco Bay Area, Urban Ore in Berkeley usually has lots of cheap electric space heaters.

Scent

Similar to sound, scent is an endless exploration. Play with different essential oils, scented flowers, incense, fruits, herbs, spices, etc. See what you like best. Often, I begin a Sure Thing with an anointing.

How to Anoint with Oils:

1. Choose a scent.

2. Hold the bottle in one hand and infuse it with your Sure Thing intention while turning the bottle in lemniscate (∞) and/or circular motions. This will mix the oil as well as your intention into it.

3. Place a few drops in the palm of your hand, then rub your palms together.

4. Bring your cupped palms to your nose and take three deep inhales.

5. Anoint your body with the oil. There's no "right" way to do this. Play with any or all of these:

- Spiral the oil onto your 3rd eye, just above the space between your eyebrows.
- Place oil on the top of your head at your crown.
- Anoint your heart by placing oil on your chest and upper back.
- Anoint your feet, belly, solar plexus, hands…
- Follow your intuition.

Now that you've anointed yourself, you may wish to anoint your beloved. To get my favorite custom blended oils for yourself, check out:

Blue Dragon Alchemy
www.bluedragonalchemy.com/store/13-moon-anointing-oils

Emerald Temple
www.emeraldtemple.com/collections/all

⭐ Deliberate Orgasm Instructions ~ The Basics ⭐

Overview

For simplicity's sake, the DOee is a female in this example. By no means are either of these roles limited to any gender.

First, let's define roles. The DOee is the person receiving a deliberate orgasm. The DOer is the person giving a deliberate orgasm. The DOer takes the DOee on a sensational ride as the DOee surrenders as much as they can. The DOee can make requests of the DOer.

By using quicker, lighter strokes, the DOer takes the DOee higher. Alternatively, slower, firmer strokes take the DOee down. The DOer determines the height of the highs and the timing of the plateaus. A plateau in sensation is created by the DOer lifting a finger or hand off of the DOee's genitals or by simply pausing. All the while, the DOee is opening, receiving, and asking for what they want.

Even though it's called a deliberate orgasm, please recall our expanded definition of orgasm: to experience pleasure moving through your body. A DO Date may include the involuntary contraction and release traditionally called orgasm or it may not. Try not to be attached to the outcome. Instead, both the DOee and the DOer may hold the intention of experiencing pleasure and/or feeling as many strokes as you can.

Get Comfortable

The DOee should get naked from the waist down, or go full monty, whatever feels best. Then, the DOee lies down in a comfortable position. The DOee may want to bow out their legs with knees bent and feet closer together. Since the priority is comfort, the DOee may want pillows under their knees and elsewhere.

The DOer situates themselves in a comfortable position next to the DOee, either lying down or sitting up. One potential posture is for the DOer to have one leg over the DOee's torso and another under their knees. Experiment with different positions and find one where you're both comfy. Because you're going to be in this position a while, use pillows and cushions for support. There are no limits on the time a DO Date can take. You may wish to set a timer, as that will provide some structure. If you do set an alarm and it goes off, but you're not ready to stop, don't. If you're using a timer, I suggest you set it for at least 8 minutes.

DOer's Observations

The DOer may begin by admiring specific aspects of the DOee's body and genitals. For example, "Your inner labia are a delicate pink color." "I like the sweeping curve from your waist to your hip." "The way your breasts spread when you lie down is so beautiful." "I'm enjoying the warmth and softness of your inner thigh."

The DOer states specific, succinct descriptions of what they observe about the DOee.

Lube Up and Stroke

The DOer gets plenty of the DOee's favorite lube on their index finger. Then, the DOer tells the DOee they are about to stroke them and that it may be a little cold. That is, unless you've warmed up the lube.

The DOer strokes and the DOee receives. If you're stroking a pussy, explore the upper left-hand quadrant of the clitoris under the hood. Some say this is the most sensational part of the clitoris. The clitoris has legs called "crura" that run beneath the outer labia in a wishbone shape. Experiment with pressure on the labia. Also, the introitus, the vaginal opening, can be pleasure inducing. Perhaps place a thumb inside or explore with varying strokes inside as well as outside. There are no rules. Discover what the most sensational part of the DOee's pussy is.

If you're stroking a cock, explore the tip and the corona, the ridge or crown that forms the rim at the very top of the penis. Also, experiment with light pressure at the base of the scrotum as you stroke the shaft. Discover what the most sensational part of the DOee's cock is.

Questions for Maximum Pleasure

The DOer may ask questions such as: Would you like a lighter stroke? Would you like a slower stroke? Do you prefer 1 (stroking in one place) or 2 (stroking in a different place)? The DOer should ask questions with simple, one-word answers.

The DOee tries to feel every stroke. If you get lost in thought, ask your DOer to pause so you can bring yourself out of your head and back into your body. No need for the DOer to lift their finger off of your clit, just stop stroking. When you are ready, ask them to begin again. Try to feel each stroke. Also, ask for exactly what you want—faster/slower stroke, different spot, firmer/lighter stroke, finger inside anus/pussy. Stay attuned to your please~o~meter with a focus on expanding pleasure.

Your goal is to experience ecstasy in the body and share this with another. The DOer is also paying attention to how their body feels with their attention primarily on their finger/hand, which is touching the DOee's genitals.

Remember, there's no agenda to climax or not to climax. The only agenda is for both of you to endeavor to feel every stroke and enjoy yourselves!

☆ Recommended Reading ☆

Befriending Your Wild Sensual Self

- *Call of the Wild: How We Heal Trauma, Awaken Our Own Power, and Use it for Good* by Kimberly Ann Johnson
- *Pronoia is the Antidote for Paranoia* by Rob Brezny ~ chapter 9
- *Women Who Run with the Wolves: Myths and Stories of the Wild Woman Archetype* by Clarissa Pinkola Estes, PhD

Dating & Relationship

- *If the Buddha Dated: A Handbook for Finding Love on a Spiritual Path* by Charlotte Karl
- *Love Worth Making: How to Have Ridiculously Great Sex in a Long-lasting Relationship* by Stephen Snyder, M.D.
- *Passionate Marriage: Keeping Love and Intimacy Alive in Committed Relationships* by David Schnarch, PhD
- *She Comes First: The Thinking Man's Guide to Pleasuring a Woman* by Ian Kerner

Falling in Love with You

- *The Body is Not an Apology* by Sonya Renee Taylor
- *Cunt: A Declaration of Independence* by Inga Muscio
- *Come as You Are: The Surprising New Science That Will Transform Your Sex Life* by Emily Nagoski, PhD
- *Madly in Love with Me: The Daring Adventure of Becoming Your Own Best Friend* by Christine Arylo
- *Reform Your Inner Mean Girl: 7 Steps to Stop Bullying Yourself and Start Loving Yourself* by Amy Ahlers and Christine Arylo

Female Anatomy & Pleasure

- *Becoming Cliterate: Why Orgasm Equality Matters–And How To Get It* by Dr. Laurie Mintz
- *The Clitoral Truth: A Secret World at Your Fingertips* by Rebecca Chalker
- *Women's Anatomy of Arousal: Secret Maps to Buried Pleasure* by Sheri Winston

Fertility Empowerment

- *Cycle Savvy: The Smart Teen's Guide to the Mysteries of Her Body* by Toni Weschler
- *Taking Charge of Your Fertility: The Definitive Guide to Natural Birth Control, Pregnancy Achievement, and Reproductive Health* by Toni Weschler

Pleasure Activism

- *Pleasure Activism: The Politics of Feeling Good* by adrienne maree brown

Spiritually Speaking

- *The 13 Moon Oracle* by Ariel Spilsbury
- *Emergence: The Shift from Ego to Essence* by Barbara Marx Hubbard
- *Home to Her* by Liz Childs Kelly
- *Magdalene Unveiled: Discover the Way of Love, Healing, and Holy Fire* by Jane Ashley
- *The Well of Truth: Stories of Spirit* by Elizabeth A. Gould
- *You Can Heal Your Life* by Louise Hay

Gratitude, Gratitude, and more Gratitude!

How do I begin to express my immense appreciation for my beloved, Bill? You are the rock in my life. You are the stability and support that gives me freedom to create. You are a magnificent human whom I learn from regularly, adore absolutely, and count my blessings every day I get to share with you. Without you, my love, the Sure Thing wouldn't be a thing. You are an incredibly devoted and loving father, son, and grandfather. You embody the sacred masculine and feminine with compassion, tenderness, and strength. I love you with all of me and treasure our life together.

My kids, Judah and Isabella. You inspire me to be courageous and share myself fully. Your encouragement for me to write this book has been a huge motivator for me. Judah, your acting as an accountability partner as we both co-work has added such a sweet dimension to our relationship. Please know that I love you both beyond words and am always here for you.

Leah, my friend, mentor, and muse, you are the first one who believed in and encouraged me to write this book. You inspired and prodded me for months, or was it years? If it wasn't for you, I would've given up. I'm certain of it. Thank you for all of your inspiration, support, and trust in my ability to do this!

A huge thanks to the group of women who participated in the Sure Thing Spring 2025 Challenge, you know who you are. I am forever grateful to you for saying "Yes!" and being part of the online course, which turned out to be the ideal structure for me to complete this book. And special thanks to my sister from another mister, Raquel, for bringing your creative genius to marketing the online course and to your breathtaking ability to capture someone's essence in a photo.

What a delight to create with Gina, the illustrator who playfully brought this book to life with her art. Thank you, Gina! Big gratitude to Marisa, my ingenious editor—you make my words sparkle! And thanks to my publisher extraordinaire, Jane Astara. Your partnership, creativity, and encouragement has brought grace and joy to this daunting endeavor.

Finally, thank you to my soul siSTARs, some of whom read early versions of the book, and all of whom supported me along the way to making this dream real, Kimberly, Bekka, Julie, Nahla, Wendy, Vyana, Ocean, Jillia, Cindy, and Ariel.

About the Author

Photo by Raquel Teitler

Elana Auerbach is a lover, mother, mentor, activist, and priestess. She spent her childhood and young adulthood on what she calls "the conveyor belt of life," being the good girl and doing what others expected of her. This looked like graduating Phi Beta Kappa from UCLA, working on Wall Street for a Japanese investment bank, and marrying someone with whom she felt no chemistry.

It all fell apart in 2001 when Elana realized she'd been living a lie and found the courage to leave her marriage. She entered a world of sensuality and sex in a San Francisco pleasure-centered community. This is where she met Bill, who would become her loverman for life.

In 2005, Elana founded "Sensuelle: A Woman's Journey into Sensuality," a program supporting women to fall in love with themselves, connect with their authentic voice, and ignite their passion. Then, in 2011, a few years after becoming an ordained priestess with the Sanctuary of the 13 Moon Mystery School, Elana was certified to teach their year-long immersion into the feminine mysteries, where she taught for over a decade.

While Elana has a wealth of professional experience guiding people deeper into their bodies and their pleasure, *The Sure Thing* comes directly from her personal life. After years of frustration and failed gimmicks to try to respark her and Bill's sex life, Elana created The Sure Thing. She wrote this book because she wants everyone to have access to this life altering practice.

Elana's writing has been featured in the *Times of London*. Follow her on Instagram and Facebook.

And follow The Sure Thing Experiment at **www.surethingexperiment.com.**

About the Illustrator

Gina Sawaya is a multi-media artist living in Oakland, California. Originally from Massachusetts, Gina has lived in California for over seven years and hopes to stay in the Bay Area. When she's not drawing and painting, she works in the environmental field and participates in multiple community activism groups. She loves spending quality time with her husband, dog, and friends.

Gina can be reached at **gina.sawaya@gmail.com.**

Endnotes

1 A Hebrew blessing of gratitude recited when doing something for the first time.

2 tinyurl.com/surethingplaylist

3 Sister priestess meaning both of us are ordained priestesses. What is a priestess? That reminds me of when my son was five years old and asked me what a priest was. "A priest is a male priestess," I said. He knew what a priestess was as he had participated in ceremonies and rituals that I'd led. Priestesses harken back to temples of old in ancient Greece, Egypt and even Jerusalem. Evidence of priestesses can be found all over the world where earth-based, matriarchal honoring traditions flourished. Since the 1990s, there has been a reemergence of the priestess in modern times. I was ordained through the Sanctuary of the 13 Moon Mystery School and my friend was ordained through the Kohenet Hebrew Priestess Institute.

4 Babylonian Talmud, Ketubot 62b

5 *The Sex-Starved Marriage* by Michelle Weiner Davis

6 adrienne maree brown coined the term "pleasure activism" in her book *Pleasure Activism: The Politics of Feeling Good.*

7 Amy Farrell, *Fat Shame: Stigma and the Fat Body in American Culture* (New York: New York University Press, 2011), 5.

8 Sabrina Springs, *Fearing the Black Body: The Racial Origins of Fat Phobia* (New York: New York University Press, 2019), 147-168.

9 Emily Nagoski, *Come As You Are: The Surprising New Science That Will Transform Your Sex Life* (New York: Simon & Schuster Paperbacks, 2021), 156-158.

10 Emily Nagoski, *Come As You Are: The Surprising New Science That Will Transform Your Sex Life* (New York: Simon & Schuster Paperbacks, 2021), 157.

11 Emily Nagoski, *Come As You Are: The Surprising New Science That Will Transform Your Sex Life* (New York: Simon & Schuster Paperbacks, 2021), 158.

12 Ian Kerner, *She Comes First: The Thinking Man's Guide to Pleasuring a Woman* (New York: HarperCollins, 2004), 17.

13 Thanks to Ariel Spilsbury for creating a profoundly healing journey to connect with the inner child that inspired this guided journey.

14 Clarissa Pinkola Estés, *Women Who Run With the Wolves: Myths and Stories of the Wild Woman Archetype* (New York: Ballantine Books, 1992), 231.

15 adrienne maree brown, *Pleasure Activism: The Politics of Feeling Good* (Chico Edinburgh: AK Press, 2019), 197.

16 Emily Nagoski, *Come As You Are: The Surprising New Science That Will Transform Your Sex Life* (New York: Simon & Schuster Paperbacks, 2021), 220.

17 Emily Nagoski, *Come As You Are: The Surprising New Science That Will Transform Your Sex Life* (New York: Simon & Schuster Paperbacks, 2021), 161.

18 Vanessa Marin, *Sex Talks: The Five Conversations That Will Transform Your Love Life* (New York: Simon Element, 2023), 6.

19 Adapted from: Stephen Snyder, *Love Worth Making: How to Have Ridiculously Great Sex in a Long-Lasting Relationship* (New York: St. Martin's Press, 2018), 193.

20 Stephen Snyder, *Love Worth Making: How to Have Ridiculously Great Sex in a Long-Lasting Relationship* (New York: St. Martin's Press, 2018), 220.

21 David Schnarch, *Passionate Marriage: Keeping Love & Intimacy Alive in Committed Relationships* (New York: Henry Holt and Company, LLC, 1997), 160.

22 Emily Nagoski, *Come As You Are: The Surprising New Science That Will Transform Your Sex Life* (New York: Simon & Schuster Paperbacks, 2021), 229.

23 Emily Nagoski, *Come As You Are: The Surprising New Science That Will Transform Your Sex Life* (New York: Simon & Schuster Paperbacks, 2021), 244.

24 Esther Perel, *Mating in Captivity: Unlocking Erotic Intelligence* (New York: HarperCollins, 2006), 185.

25 Maria Uloko, MD, "The Surprising Link Between Sex and Longevity," *VELLA Bioscience* (June 2025): https://vellabio.com/blogs/vella-voice/link-between-sex-and-longevity.

26 Chao Cao, MPH, Lin Yang, PhD, Tianlin Xu, MPH, Patricia A. Cavazos-Rehg, PhD, "Trends in Sexual Activity and Associations with All-Cause and Cause-Specific Mortality Among US Adults," Journal of Sexual Medicine, Volume 17, Issue 10, (October 2020): 1903–1913, https://doi.org/10.1016/j.jsxm.2020.05.028.

27 tinyurl.com/surethingplaylist

Visit us at

www.floweroflifepress.com

www.ingramcontent.com/pod-product-compliance
Lightning Source LLC
Chambersburg PA
CBHW081210130726
47997CB00009B/2611